Two Nations, One Money?

*Canada's Monetary System
following a Quebec Secession*

David E.W. Laidler
and William B.P. Robson

with
Lloyd C. Atkinson, John Grant,
William M. Scarth, and Bernard Fortin

The Canada Round:
A Series on the Economics of
the Breakup of Confederation — No. 3

John McCallum, Series Editor

C.D. Howe Institute

C.D. Howe Institute publications are available from:

Renouf Publishing Company Limited, 1294 Algoma Road,
Ottawa, Ontario K1B 3W8; phone (613) 741-4333; fax (613) 741-5439

and from Renouf's stores at:

61 Sparks Street, Ottawa (613) 238-8985
211 Yonge Street, Toronto (416) 363-3171

For trade book orders, please contact:

McGraw-Hill Ryerson Limited, 300 Water Street,
Whitby, Ontario L1N 9B6; phone (416) 430-5050

Institute publications are also available in microform from:

Micromedia Limited, 20 Victoria Street, Toronto, Ontario M5C 2N8

This book is printed on recycled, acid-free paper.

Canadian Cataloguing in Publication Data

Laidler, David, 1938–
    Two nations, one money?

(The Canada round ; no. 3)
ISBN 0-88806-286-9

1. Money – Canada. 2. Money – Quebec (Province).
3. Currency question – Canada. 4. Currency question – Quebec (Province).
5. Monetary unions. 6. Federal-provincial relations – Canada.
7. Quebec (Province) – History – Autonomy and independence movements.
I. Robson, William B. P. (William Bertie Provost), 1959–
II. C.D. Howe Institute. III. Title. IV. Series.

HG655.L35 1991   332.4'971   C91-095368-6

7332/

Contents

Foreword v

The Study in Brief vii

*The View from Bélanger-Campeau: Monetary Options
of a Sovereign Quebec,* a summary by *William B.P. Robson* xi

*Two Nations, One Money? Canada's Monetary
System following a Quebec Secession,*
by *David E.W. Laidler and William B.P. Robson*

Chapter 1:
Introduction 3
The Nation-State and the Currency Area 3
The Issues to Be Discussed 4

Chapter 2:
Some General Principles 7
The Functions of Money 7
Why Do Separate Currencies Exist? 10

Chapter 3:
The Principles Applied 14
Possible Post-Breakup Monetary Arrangements .14
A Disintegration of the Monetary Union 16
Maintaining the Monetary Union 24
Continued Monetary Union Benefits Both Sides .32

Chapter 4:
The Political Dimension and the Dynamics of Breakup 33
The Complementarity of Economic and Monetary Union 33
The Credibility of SQ's Commitment to the Monetary Union 34
Concluding Comment 37

Appendix A:
Data Sources and Calculations 39
Transactions Costs of Separate Currencies 39
Seigniorage 41
The Size of the Economy and the
    Variability of Real Exchange Rates 46
The Costs of a Divided Clearing System 46

Appendix B:
Should Canada Have Its Own Dollar? 48
Eliminating Transactions Costs
    between the Canadian and U.S. Dollars 48
Accepting the U.S. Inflation Rate 49
Loss of Seigniorage 50
Loss of the Bank of Canada as Lender of Last Resort 50
Greater Vulnerability to External Shocks 51
The Credibility of the Canadian Dollar 51

A Comment, by *Lloyd C. Atkinson* 53

A Comment, by *John Grant* 57

A Note on the Desirability of a
    Separate Quebec Currency, by *William M. Scarth* 65

A Comment, by *Bernard Fortin* 77

The Contributors 83

Members of the C.D. Howe Institute 85

Foreword

Canada appears poised to embark on an historic political reconfiguration. It is essential that this process be undertaken with a clear and widely diffused understanding of the wellspring of Canadians' economic prosperity.

With that in mind, the C.D. Howe Institute is publishing this series of monographs entitled *The Canada Round*. The series assembles the work of many of Canada's leading economic and political analysts. The monographs are organized into two groups. The first group, called "The Economics of Constitutional Renewal", rests on the assumption of renewed federalism and is organized around economic themes. It examines the economic goals that Canadians have set for themselves, as well as the means of achieving them and the influence of alternative constitutional structures.

The second group of studies, called "The Economics of the Breakup of Confederation", examines the economic consequences of Quebec independence for both Quebec and the rest of Canada. A unique feature of the studies in the second group is that they will be integrated with the research that has already been carried out by Quebec's Bélanger-Campeau Commission. Where appropriate, each of the studies in this group will include a summary of the relevant analysis by the Bélanger-Campeau Commission, contributions by experts from across Canada, as well as shorter critiques or replies. This format, we believe, will help to pierce Canada's "several solitudes" and create a pan-Canadian meeting of minds.

The Canada Round is not intended to alarm or frighten — the process of collective political definition will turn on more than simply questions of dollars and cents. And, as these monographs will reveal, economics rarely produces an open-and-shut case as to the superiority of one possible set of rules over another. Even if it could do this, it would be unwise to assume that economic analysis alone could change the minds of those who are committed to a particular vision of the political future.

It is equally clear, however, that Canadians are now seeking greater understanding of the links between the economy, the Constitution, and legal and political life. A significant reform of the Constitution will influence the economy, in some cases for the better; a rending of the Constitution under conditions of acrimony will almost certainly damage it. Thus, the purpose of the series is to help Canadians think constructively about the benefits and costs of alternative constitutional designs.

Underlying the monographs is a focus on the economic well-being of Canadians, both now and in the future. To best insure this over the immediate future, Canada needs calm, open negotiations in which efforts are made to understand and incorporate the aspirations of all participants. This series of monographs is dedicated to that effort.

John McCallum, the series editor and Chairman of the Department of Economics at McGill University, organized the intellectual input. Within the C.D. Howe Institute, David Brown, Senior Policy Analyst, played a coordinating role. This third monograph in the series was copy edited by Barry A. Norris and desktop published by Brenda Palmer. As with all C.D. Howe Institute publications, the analysis and views presented here are the responsibility of the authors and do not necessarily reflect the opinions of the Institute's members or Board of Directors.

Thomas E. Kierans
President and
Chief Executive Officer

The Study in Brief

If Quebec were to separate from Canada, what kind of monetary system would be in the best economic interests of the two parties? What kind of monetary system would actually emerge? Two very different questions — with two very different sets of answers.

What Would Be Best?

On this first question, there is unanimity. The principal authors, David Laidler and William Robson, argue that maintaining the Canadian monetary union, with a jointly governed central bank and a common financial system, would be the best economic option for both Quebec and "the Rest of Canada" (ROC). None of the four discussants offers any disagreement with this proposition, which is also very widely accepted in Quebec. This first-best option amounts to minimizing changes to the current system. The result would be very close to the status quo, except that Quebec would have formal representation on the board of the Bank of Canada and would be entitled to its share of the Bank's "profits", or seigniorage.

The second-best option, according to Laidler and Robson, would be for a sovereign Quebec (SQ) to continue using the Canadian dollar but without having any influence over Canadian monetary policy. They argue that ROC could not stop SQ from using the Canadian dollar — except at great cost to both itself and SQ — but that there would be advantages to both sides from cooperating with each other.

Laidler and Robson consider two other options. From the standpoints of both ROC and SQ, the worst possible option would be a separate SQ currency with a floating exchange rate. The second-worst option would be a separate SQ currency pegged to either the

U.S. or the Canadian dollar.* The biggest problem with both of these options concerns issues of credibility. It would take some time for SQ to establish its reputation in financial markets, and in the meantime there may be problems involving risk premiums on interest rates, possible capital flight out of SQ, and competitive devaluations of the SQ currency. At least in the short run, such competitive devaluations (or depreciations) would make ROC industry less competitive, U.S. industry more protectionist, and the Quebec economy more inflationary. A new SQ currency, which would be a move in the opposite direction from what is now occurring in Europe, would also increase the transactions costs of carrying on trade between SQ and ROC.

While the various authors differ on certain points of nuance, there seems to be broad consensus on these issues both in Quebec and elsewhere in Canada. William Scarth, for example, agrees with the basic points of the essay by Laidler and Robson, although he is less confident regarding the capacity of the Bank of Canada to deliver a lower inflation rate than the U.S. monetary authorities. Bernard Fortin raises questions regarding competitive devaluations and seigniorage. Lloyd Atkinson and John Grant are more concerned with the second of our questions.

What Would Happen?

> If ROC and SQ remained on such friendly terms that they could negotiate the preservation of the Canadian common market and monetary union as it now exists, it is hard to see why their friendship could not be extended to preserving some sort of political union as well.
>
> – Laidler and Robson

This second question involves the degree of acrimony that would accompany a breakup and it is at least possible that the amount of

---

* However, as Lloyd Atkinson points out in his comment, for practical purposes, the rate of exchange of a separate SQ currency might have to be "fixed to the U.S. dollar, because it is not apparent that there would remain a ROC and, therefore, a ROC dollar to which it could be fixed."

cooperation needed to achieve the first-best solution would not exist. Laidler and Robson raise the specter of a vicious circle based on the lack of credibility of SQ's commitment to the maintenance of the monetary union. Even those Quebecers who have complete confidence in the good intentions of the SQ government would be influenced by their perceptions of the expectations of other economic agents. Fears that SQ might launch a new currency could precipitate an exodus of money from Quebec, a major credit crunch, and a greater chance that the SQ government would feel pushed into issuing its own currency.

On a similar theme, John Grant points to Canada's huge debt as a source of vulnerability if creditors begin to worry about the creditworthiness of a fractured country. Lloyd Atkinson asks whether foreign *and* domestic creditors will "want to play in the traffic while Canadians sort out these matters" and whether they might not choose to park their investments elsewhere.

In the context of a currency crisis, Atkinson asks whether SQ would cede complete sovereignty over monetary policy to ROC — especially "if the financial-market outcome of the breakup of the country resulted in a heavily indebted Quebec having to endure punishingly high interest rates." He thinks not, and, like Laidler and Robson, argues that we might well end up with a separate SQ currency, even though this would be in no one's economic interests.

In a thoughtful response to these issues, Fortin invokes a number of factors, including the economic interests of the SQ government and the current globalizing trends in the world, to argue that such pessimistic scenarios are unlikely.

It seems, then, that economists can achieve a fine consensus on the technical issues involved in our first question: What would be best? We are much less certain when it comes to the question of what would actually happen amid the political and economic dynamics that would be unleashed by a breakup of Canada.

John McCallum
Series Editor

The View from Bélanger-Campeau: Monetary Options of a Sovereign Quebec

a summary by
William B.P. Robson

This is a brief digest of Bernard Fortin, "Les options monétaires d'un Québec souverain," in Quebec, Commission on the Political and Constitutional Future of Quebec [Bélanger-Campeau Commission], *Éléments d'analyse économique pertinents à la révision du statut politique et constitutionnel du Québec* [Background papers], vol. 1 (Quebec, 1991). It summarizes the views expressed by Fortin in his paper, and does not represent the views expressed by the Commission in its report.

Introduction

This paper examines the costs and benefits of various monetary options for a sovereign Quebec (SQ), starting from the assumption that SQ and "the Rest of Canada" (ROC) will maintain a system of free movement of people, goods, and capital between them. Four main possibilities are canvassed, ranging from complete monetary integration to complete disintegration:

1. Monetary union, with or without an SQ voice in the setting of monetary policy;
2. A separate SQ currency fixed to the ROC dollar (termed a "pseudo monetary union");

3. A separate SQ currency fixed to the U.S. dollar; and
4. A separate SQ currency with a floating exchange rate.

Under the first option, the government of SQ would declare the ROC currency to be legal tender in SQ. Given the integration of financial institutions across the borders, it would be natural to harmonize SQ's regulation of the financial sector with that of ROC.

There are at least two possibilities for the setting of monetary policy under this option: a new central bank under joint control of SQ and ROC (with shared seigniorage); and an arrangement whereby the ROC central bank continues to run monetary policy and SQ banks maintain reserves with it. The former scenario is compared with the West African monetary union and the proposals for the Eurofed, the latter with Ireland between 1921 and 1928.

The Costs of a Separate Currency for SQ

In two of its functions — a unit of account and medium of exchange — the usefulness of money grows with the extent of its use. A separate SQ currency would impose three types of costs: transactions costs, accounting and record-keeping costs, and costs related to exchange-rate risk — costs that would increase with the degree of SQ's monetary independence from ROC.

Based on estimates of transactions and accounting costs associated with separate currencies in the European Community and modified to reflect the transactions costs Quebec already incurs in its dealings with trading partners apart from other Canadian provinces, such costs might amount to 0.6 percent of GDP annually in SQ's case. ROC would also be subject to such costs in its dealings with SQ. To the extent that exchange-rate risk translates into interest-rate premiums, the adverse impact on capital accumulation could be expected to reduce economic growth over the long run. The adoption of a separate currency would have an adverse effect on economic efficiency analogous to that of trade barriers; it is, therefore, at odds with the principle of maintaining a common market.

The Advantages of a Separate Currency for SQ

A common currency would, however, impose costs on SQ in the form of constraints on its monetary and exchange-rate policy and its ability to finance government expenditure through money creation.

As far as the first of these is concerned, in the short run, even a separate currency will provide no benefit, since it would have to be maintained at a fixed rate against the ROC dollar for a considerable period of time in a pseudo monetary union.[1] Over the longer run, a separate currency will help the Quebec economy absorb certain types of shocks. But many of the long-run advantages that are widely perceived to flow from a separate currency are illusory. The extent to which changes in monetary policy will have effects on the real economy depends on the credibility of policymakers and the process by which economic agents form expectations, both of which are volatile and ill-understood. Much more reliable is monetary policy's influence on the rate of inflation. Accordingly, given the damage that inflation does to the economy, monetary policy should be oriented toward long-run price stability.

The ability to substitute money creation for other types of taxation in financing government expenditure is also a questionable benefit. Other, less damaging — and more democratic — types of taxes are available. Moreover, access to this type of financing tends to undermine budgetary discipline.

Therefore, the main potential benefit on the monetary policy front for SQ in having its own currency comes down to the opportunity to run a more stable and less inflationary policy than that of

---

1 Fortin notes a minor benefit from a separate currency: the superior knowledge of Quebec's own financial system that would flow from observations on separate monetary aggregates.

the Bank of ROC. Since Canada's inflation rate has not been very high in recent years, while the Bank of Canada has been pursuing an anti-inflationary strategy, this may not be a very important benefit. In any event, it is not clear that the SQ authorities would choose such a route, given the temptation for politicians to run inflationary policies for short-run benefit.

A further benefit arises from the ability to absorb external shocks through exchange-rate movements. Leaving aside competitive devaluations in response to shocks affecting SQ and ROC similarly, which would be inconsistent with the concept of a common market and might provoke reprisals, the relevant scenario is one in which a flexible exchange rate helps SQ adjust to a shock that affects it and ROC differently. But the evident flexibility of interprovincial terms of trade and factor mobility between provinces mean that the advantage of a flexible exchange rate in this context may not be very large. In addition, the Quebec economy is small enough that the money illusion on which the adjustment-easing property of a flexible exchange rate depends may be weak. In any event, various fiscal measures for promoting adjustments — to the extent that they are compatible with international trade agreements — will be available to SQ.

A Monetary Union with the United States

The option of an SQ currency tied to the U.S. dollar demands attention to several points:

- monetary and economic union go together, and Canada and the United States still have important barriers, particularly to labor, between them;
- Quebec trades more with other parts of Canada than with the United States;
- The transition costs of switching to a currency pegged to the U.S. dollar would be much higher for SQ than a continued link to ROC;

- it is likely — though not certain — that external shocks will affect the SQ and ROC economies more symmetrically than the SQ and U.S. economies;
- proponents of a such a step should demonstrate that U.S. monetary policy is and will be less inflationary than the Bank of Canada's; and
- monetary union with the United States would not permit SQ to import lower U.S. interest rates.

These considerations favor an SQ-ROC over an SQ-U.S. monetary union. A further possibility, however, would be an SQ-ROC union with an exchange rate fixed to the U.S. dollar, which would be a step toward an eventual North American common market.

Conclusion

An SQ-ROC monetary union would be the best option, on the basis of the numerous benefits it would confer on SQ. Such an arrangement would also benefit ROC. The benefits that SQ would forego in maintaining a currency union with ROC would be limited. A separate SQ currency pegged to the ROC dollar is an unattractive option, involving many of the costs, but almost none of the benefits of an independent currency. And, although a separate currency pegged to the U.S. dollar would be a viable option for SQ, it is less attractive than a continued link with ROC.

Two Nations, One Money?

*Canada's Monetary System
following a Quebec Secession*

David E.W. Laidler
and William B.P. Robson

Chapter 1

Introduction

The Nation-State and the Currency Area

Nation-states are political entities. Currency areas, on the other hand, are economic entities. National political and currency area boundaries usually — though not invariably — coincide. This is because a monetary system will not quite run itself. It needs a government — traditionally, a national one — to oversee certain aspects of its operation. Thus, at present, the geographic area in which the Canadian dollar circulates coincides with that over which the government of Canada exercises political power. The Canadian monetary union is overseen by the Bank of Canada, which derives its authority from an act of the Canadian federal Parliament, and the federal government has substantial nationwide power over other areas of policy affecting the functioning of the monetary union.

Canada's current constitutional crisis raises the possibility that this arrangement may not endure. A large segment of Quebec's population would like powers over such matters as language, culture, and immigration — currently exercised by, or shared with, the federal government — turned over to Quebec. Efforts to resolve these problems within a renewed federal system are now under way, and we earnestly hope that they succeed. But if they do not, and Quebec assumes the status of a sovereign state, then a whole array of difficult questions about political and economic organization arise. Among these are questions about what would, or should, become of the Canadian monetary union, and in whose hands the relevant decisions would lie.

In this essay, we develop answers to these questions. We argue that the nature of the monetary arrangements likely to accompany the separation of Quebec would depend heavily on whether the breakup of the Canadian federation was amicably arranged or not and on whether Quebec would accept those limits on its sovereignty needed to ensure the stability of the monetary union. Since a breakup, if it occurs, seems unlikely to be amicable, the array of politically possible outcomes is somewhat narrower than the array of technically feasible ones — not least because the less amicable the breakup, the less willing an independent Quebec will be to accept limits on its sovereignty, and the less willing other parts of Canada would be to accommodate Quebec in these areas.[1] In particular, we conclude that — although the monetary union might survive — it is distinctly possible that the political dynamics of a breakup could be fatal to the union even though no one actively sought such an outcome, at considerable economic cost to the inhabitants of all of what is now Canada.

The Issues to Be Discussed

In the following pages, we initially set aside judgments about what is and is not likely to be politically possible, and consider the economics of a wide array of technically feasible arrangements. We begin by discussing the benefits and costs that arise from the use of a common currency, and show how they interact with other aspects of economic integration. In the light of this analysis, we then consider the range of potential monetary arrangements between a sovereign Quebec (SQ)[2] and a still-united "Rest of Canada" (ROC), evaluating

---

1 Tom Courchene argues that, in many areas, an independent Quebec would find its freedom of action *more* constrained than the province of Quebec is within Confederation. See Thomas J. Courchene, *In Praise of Renewed Federalism,*The Canada Round 2 (Toronto: C.D. Howe Institute, 1991).

2 Our use of a somewhat jarring acronym, SQ, to refer to a post-secession Quebec arises from our wish to avoid constant use of such adjectives as "pre-independence" and "post-independence" and our desire to emphasize that the new entity would differ in important ways from the existing Canadian province of Quebec. Just as it is misleading to refer to the truncated post-secession "Rest of Canada" as Canada, so it is misleading to refer to the other secession state as "Quebec", as though nothing fundamental had changed.

their desirability from the perspectives of the economic interests of both sides.

We argue that, particularly from SQ's point of view, the option of a separate SQ currency with a flexible exchange rate would be so risky as to be extremely unattractive. We point out, however, that SQ could introduce a separate currency and *fix* its exchange rate. If, as is quite possible, the SQ exchange rate were to be fixed at an artificially low level against ROC's currency (hereafter referred to as the ROC dollar), this would inflict considerable short-term economic damage on ROC; it might also impose important long-term costs on SQ because of the domestic inflation it could generate there.

Maintaining the monetary union, on the other hand, would prevent the emergence of considerable transactions costs between the two parties, and might be expected to reduce the damage to the creditworthiness of both sides in the eyes of the rest of the world arising from Quebec's separation. If cooperation in central banking and other aspects of the financial system could be maintained, despite the restrictions on the sovereignty of both sides involved, this option would be all the more favorable to the economic interests of both SQ and ROC.

We also consider whose choice it is to maintain the monetary union. As far as actions by governments are concerned, we argue that, while ROC could take actions that reduce the benefits to SQ of using the ROC dollar — actions that would inflict damage on ROC as well as on SQ — it is, from a technical point of view, up to SQ whether or not it remains within the monetary union. The actions that the government of ROC would need to take to *prevent* SQ from doing so — namely, the introduction of comprehensive foreign-exchange controls — seem beyond the bounds of political possibility.

Despite both parties' strong economic interest in cooperating to maintain the monetary union, however, these considerations could easily be overridden by the political and confidence-related dynamics of an acrimonious separation. The actions of individuals and businesses in financial markets could produce circumstances in which even an SQ government initially strongly committed to the monetary union would find it attractive to abandon the arrangement. In this case, the most probable monetary outcome of a breakup of the Canadian federation would be the economically damaging emergence of two separate currencies, with that of SQ pegged at an artificially low level against that of ROC.

Chapter 2

Some General Principles

The Functions of Money

Discussion of the monetary union involves an institution, money, that is so basic to the functioning of Canada's economy and Canadian society that it is often taken for granted. It is therefore helpful to start by reviewing money's uses. Money, we are often told, is a unit of account, a means of exchange, and a store of value. As Bernard Fortin points out, in considering the economic benefits generated by a monetary system, the first two of these functions are vital.[1]

Money as a Unit of Account

In Canada, prices of goods and services offered for sale are stated in terms of an entity called the "Canadian dollar". Incomes, being the result of sales of goods and services, are usually computed in Canadian dollars, as are profit and loss statements and company balance sheets. So are tax liabilities and debt contracts. Contracts regarding debts and matters such as pension obligations, which involve commitments to make and receive payments in the future, illustrate a particular — and, in the context of the subject of this paper, crucial

---

1 Bernard Fortin, "Les options monétaires d'un Québec souverain," in Quebec, Commission on the Political and Constitutional Future of Quebec [Bélanger-Campeau Commission], *Éléments d'analyse économique pertinents à la révision du statut politique et constitutionnel du Québec* [Background papers], vol. 1 (Quebec, 1991), p. 287.

— aspect of money's unit-of-account role: its function as a standard of deferred payment.[2]

At one time, the Canadian dollar represented a certain weight of gold, and to state prices in dollars was, in fact, to announce rates at which goods and services would be exchanged against gold. Nowadays, however, it is a completely abstract entity. Prices stated in terms of dollars only attain concrete meaning when compared with one another — apples at one dollar a kilogram and oranges at two dollars a kilogram involves an exchange ratio (or relative price) of one kilogram of oranges for two of apples, and so on.

An abstract unit of account is an immensely productive social institution. The common use of the dollar simplifies the communication of price information and facilitates the recordkeeping on which so many economic decisions within the Canadian monetary system depend.

Money as a Means of Exchange

Canadians are also willing to accept, as a result of social convention reinforced by legal tender laws, coins and Bank of Canada notes denominated in various multiples of dollars in exchange for goods and services and in discharge of debts. There are also bank deposits, denominated in Canadian dollars, that banks stand ready to redeem in Bank of Canada currency. To the extent that they are transferable by cheque, these too function as means of exchange.

Even in 1991 there is no better way of driving home the importance of this function of money — so commonplace that it usually goes unnoticed — than to quote the opening paragraph of William Stanley Jevons' once widely used 1874 textbook, *Money and the Mechanism of Exchange*:

---

2 Students of monetary economics may find the omission here of money's role as a store of value odd. What matters for the arguments presented below, however, is the existence of a wide range of stores of value denominated in terms of the unit of account, not just of the small subset which — also being means of exchange — is money in that sense.

Some years since, Mademoiselle Zélie, a singer of the Théatre Lyrique at Paris, made a professional tour round the world, and gave a concert in the Society Islands. In exchange for an air from Norma and a few other songs, she was to receive a third part of the receipts. When counted, her share was found to consist of three pigs, twenty-three turkeys, forty-four chickens, five thousand cocoa-nuts, besides considerable quantities of bananas, lemons, and oranges. At the Halle in Paris...this amount of live stock and vegetables might have brought four thousand francs, which would have been good remuneration for five songs. In the Society Islands, however, pieces of money were very scarce; and as Mademoiselle could not consume any considerable portion of the receipts herself, it became necessary in the mean time to feed the pigs and poultry with the fruit.

Being willing to accept Canadian dollar currency and cheques drawn on Canadian dollar bank accounts, Canadians can also count on using them to make payments to others. This social convention immeasurably facilitates market activity, permitting Canadians to avoid barter transactions and to sell things at one time and place, secure in the knowledge that what they receive in exchange will be readily accepted when, at another time and place, they decide to buy something.

The Relationship between Money's Functions

Although the arrangement is often taken for granted, nothing logically requires that Canada's (or any other country's) means of exchange be denominated in terms of its unit of account. Canadians could, for example, keep their books and state prices in U.S. dollars, and consummate transactions using local currency. Indeed, a separation of this sort sometimes occurs in economies subject to rapid inflation, when buyers and sellers take to quoting prices in (usually) U.S. dollars even though local currency, valued at the current exchange rate, continues to be used to close transactions.

Separating money's roles as a unit of account and a means of exchange, however, gives rise to extra computation costs. At the moment when each transaction actually occurs, the agreed price in terms of the unit of account has to be transformed into a price in terms of the means of exchange. If this cumbersome expedient avoids other costs — such as losses that would arise from stating prices in terms of a rapidly depreciating currency — all is well and good. In the absence of inflation, though, considerable convenience stems from stating prices in terms of the currency that will be accepted or offered in exchange and from keeping accounts in the same terms. That is why, in conditions of reasonable price stability, the simpler arrangement usually prevails.

Why Do Separate Currencies Exist?

Since the benefits of using a common money as a unit of account and a means of exchange arise because money reduces the frictions involved in market activity, it would seem that the right number of monies for any market is one. Why, then, to the extent that their market activities extend beyond national borders, should citizens of any country not choose to belong to some supranational monetary union encompassing the wider market in which they participate — in Canada's case, for example, by opting to use the U.S. dollar? The maintenance of a separate currency offers four types of benefits to a country.

To Control Inflation

The most important power conferred by a separate currency is control of the inflation rate, through the central bank's influence over the rate at which money is created. At one time, it was widely believed that there was a long-term tradeoff between inflation and unemployment, and that monetary policy could be used judiciously to increase employment and, perhaps, economic growth. Nowadays, the expansionary effects of higher inflation on employment are generally considered to be transient at best and perhaps negative in the long run, and the importance of price stability as a long-term objective of monetary policy has come increasingly to the fore.

Regardless of one's views on this matter, inflation is of political concern to citizens, and it is therefore desirable to vest control over it in an institution answerable to them. This does not imply that the day-to-day conduct of monetary policy should be under the direct control of elected politicians.[3] It does imply, however, that elected representatives should have ultimate political responsibility for monetary policy's long-run stance, through the power to appoint and reappoint central bank officials, perhaps through the power to override such officials' authority by way of written directives where there are serious disagreements, and, above all, through parliamentary authority over the legislation subject to which monetary policy is executed.

To Obtain the Benefits of Seigniorage

A government that controls its own money benefits from "seigniorage" — the profits made from the creation of money. A country that did not have its own currency would forego seigniorage as a source of revenue; instead, the seigniorage would be collected by the monetary authority of the country whose money was used. Seigniorage is a significant source of government revenue: in Canada last year, the federal government's financial position was improved by roughly $2.6 billion as a consequence of its ownership of the Bank of Canada and the Royal Canadian Mint.[4]

To Cope with a Financial Crisis

A separate currency also increases the power of a central government to deal with a financial crisis. In the event of a run on deposits

---

3 There is, in fact, a good deal to be said against an arrangement of this sort. See David E.W. Laidler, *How Shall We Govern the Governor? A Critique of the Governance of the Bank of Canada*, The Canada Round 1 (Toronto: C.D. Howe Institute, 1991).

4 For a more detailed discussion of seigniorage, see Appendix A.

induced by the public's loss of confidence in the banking system, for example, the central bank is able to play the role of lender of last resort, injecting newly created money into the system to restore confidence and relieve the crisis. A country that does not maintain monetary independence must maintain an institution well enough endowed with foreign currency assets and/or gold to play such a role, or depend on the central bank of the country whose currency it uses to come to its help in a crisis — a situation calculated to promote the sort of uncertainty that makes the occurrence of bank runs more likely.

A separate currency offers additional benefits in the event of a widespread loss of confidence in an economy, particularly one involving a flight of capital from the country. It makes capital controls easier to impose by permitting convertibility between the domestic and foreign currencies to be suspended. And it opens the possibility of a devaluation that improves the relative prices of domestic assets and the competitive position of producers of tradable goods and services sufficiently to staunch the flow of funds abroad.

To Adjust More Easily to Real Shocks

A separate currency offers one further advantage provided that its exchange rate is left free to vary in response to market forces. "Real" shocks to the economy, such as declines in demand for exports or increased domestic competition from imports, require a downward adjustment in the *real* exchange rate — that is, the relationship between domestic wages and prices and those prevailing abroad. If a country shares a currency with — or maintains an exchange rate irrevocably fixed on — another country whose economy is affected differently by such a shock, adjustment in the real exchange rate will involve changes in nominal prices and wages in markets for specific goods and types of labor. To the extent that nominal wages and prices adjust sluggishly to changes in market conditions, however, downward adjustments in the real exchange rate in the face of negative real shocks will involve temporary — but often sizable — losses of output and employment.

If, on the other hand, the country maintains a separate currency whose *nominal* exchange rate is free to move, then a change in its external value can help the transition. Because prices in the foreign-exchange market adjust more quickly and easily than prices in labor markets, for example, adjustment in the real exchange rate by this route is usually smoother and less prone to generate transitional unemployment. Significantly, however, this advantage is less important in smaller, more specialized economies. In such economies, individuals and businesses find it easier to recognize the effects on their income and wealth implied by changes in world markets, and hence are readier to adjust wages and prices in response to them. Larger, more complex economies, where individuals and businesses find the required responses harder to calibrate, benefit more from exchange-rate flexibility, because the foreign-exchange market makes at least part of the adjustment on their behalf.

Chapter 3

The Principles Applied

It is now time to turn to the potential monetary consequences of a breakup of the Canadian federation and to examine them in light of the principles just laid out. It is worth emphasizing at the outset that, while the scenarios can be ranked in terms of their compatibility with more or less acrimonious breakups, our intention at this stage is simply to canvass possibilities in as much detail as the speculative nature of this exercise allows. We defer discussion of the probabilities of the various outcomes to the next chapter.

Possible Post-Breakup Monetary Arrangements

The question of what sort of monetary arrangement between a sovereign Quebec (SQ) and "the Rest of Canada" (ROC) might follow a breakup has already generated a literature: it was discussed during the debate that preceded the 1980 Quebec referendum on sovereignty-association, and it has attracted renewed interest since the failure of the Meech Lake Accord.[1] There is considerable agree-

---

1 See, in addition to Bernard Fortin's study for the Bélanger-Campeau Commission summarized in this volume, two research reports prepared for the Quebec Ministry of Intergovernmental Affairs in 1978: Bernard Fortin, "Les avantages et les coûts des différentes options monétaires d'une petite économie ouverte: un cadre analytique"; and Henri-Paul Rousseau, "Unions monétaires et monnaies nationales: une étude économique de quelques cas historiques." See also Henri-Paul Rousseau, "L'intégration politique: est-elle nécessaire à l'intégration moné-taire?" in Claude Montmarquette et al., *Économie du Québec et choix politiques* (Montréal: Les Presses de l'Université du Québec, 1979); and David E.W. Laidler, *Money after Meech*, C.D. Howe Institute Commentary 22 (Toronto: C.D. Howe Institute, 1990).

ment in this literature about what options are and are not economically viable, and about their relative merits from SQ's standpoint. Four possible options are generally discussed:

1. a separate SQ currency with a floating exchange rate;
2. a separate SQ currency pegged to either the ROC or the U.S. dollar;
3. continued use of the ROC dollar by SQ, with no SQ representation in the setting of monetary policy; or
4. continued use of the ROC dollar by SQ, with SQ representation in the setting of monetary policy.

The greater the degree of acrimony involved in the breakup, the more complete the disintegration of the monetary union is likely to be. In the event of an acrimonious disintegration, currently expressed good intentions about preserving the Canadian economic union are likely to come under attack from interest groups in both SQ and ROC who would find their pleas for special treatment falling on ears made receptive by nationalist rhetoric. To the degree that the economic union is thus undermined by political acrimony, the preservation of the monetary union is likely to be threatened also, both because an impaired economic union would lessen the attractiveness of a monetary union and because disputes in one area are likely to spill over into disputes into other areas, even those that were initially uncontentious.

Speaking broadly, options 1 and 2 appear to be the results most likely to follow a hostile breakup that made it politically difficult for SQ and ROC to accept the limits on their sovereignty necessary to preserve the union. Option 4 is easier to envisage as the result of an amicable parting. Option 3 contains two separate sub-scenarios that are also orderable in terms of their compatibility with a more or less friendly outcome: a shared currency with unintegrated financial systems — that is, separate clearing systems, regulatory regimes, and deposit insurance schemes — (less friendly); and a shared currency with an integrated financial system (more friendly).

A Disintegration
of the Monetary Union

The Canadian monetary union would disintegrate most completely if SQ were to establish its own currency and allow its value to fluctuate freely in the foreign-exchange market. Technically speaking, the steps involved in moving to such an arrangement are straightforward, if complicated in some of their details.

A Separate SQ Currency with a Floating Exchange Rate

Newly printed SQ currency would be issued by a newly created SQ central bank. The new currency would be accompanied by laws requiring it to be used within SQ for the calculation and payment of taxes, and making it legal tender in private transactions — that is, the medium that, aside from legally enforceable contracts specifying some other medium of payment, creditors *would have to* accept in discharge of debts. The SQ central bank would require SQ financial institutions to maintain reserves and/or settlement balances with it — perhaps with SQ currency and deposits newly created for the purpose — through which it would regulate the internal value of the currency. And, unless it contemplated a completely clean float, the SQ government would need to endow the SQ central bank with reserves of foreign exchange (ROC dollars, U.S. dollars, and other currencies) to use in regulating the external value of the currency.[2]

In this scenario, SQ would gain control over its own inflation rate. As Bernard Fortin remarks, it is not clear that the pursuit of price stability would be an important consideration for SQ politicians, but if price stability is to be SQ's objective — and a number of sub-

---

2 It is conceivable that part of these reserves could be SQ's share of the foreign-exchange reserves of the Bank of Canada. Given the acrimony that would attend this scenario, however, this possibility seems highly unlikely.

missions to the Bélanger-Campeau Commission stressed this goal[3] — it is hard to see how an SQ central bank could be any more tenacious in its pursuit of this goal than the Bank of Canada is at present. Hence, on this front, SQ would appear to have little to gain from creating its own currency.

If it instituted its own currency, however, the SQ government would receive seigniorage from the SQ central bank and mint. Since, under such arrangements, the central bank would have unrestricted power to create assets for SQ financial institutions to hold, it would also be able to act as lender of last resort to the SQ banking system in the event of a crisis. The SQ government would also acquire additional tools to employ in combating a capital flight.

SQ could also benefit from the capacity of a flexible exchange rate to cushion the economy from real shocks. As noted earlier, however, the usefulness of this mechanism is positively related to the size of an economy and negatively related to its openness to international trade. Evidence seems to suggest that factor price differentials with trading partners that are out of line with nominal exchange rates persist only about two-thirds as long in Quebec-sized economies as in Canada-sized economies (see Appendix A). This result is consistent with our view that the capacity of a flexible exchange rate to absorb real shocks might not be very significant for SQ, although it obviously stops a long way short of proving the point.

Against these advantages, however, must be set an important disadvantage. An SQ with its own flexible-exchange-rate currency would be faced with substantial new costs in its external transactions. Foreign exchange would have to be bought and sold in connection with every act of importing, exporting, borrowing, or

---

3 See Fortin, "Les avantages et les coûts"; and Daniel Racette, "Intégration financière internationale et interdépendance des politiques macro-économiques nationales," in Quebec, Commission on the Political and Constitutional Future of Quebec [Bélanger-Campeau Commission], *Éléments d'analyse économique pertinents à la révision du statut politique et constitutionnel du Québec* [Background papers], vol. 1 (Quebec, 1991).

lending between SQ and ROC. Financial transactions costs alone related to such an arrangement would likely amount to at least 0.14 percent of combined ROC-SQ GDP, or some $1 billion annually in 1991 dollars — of which roughly half would be borne by SQ. Bernard Fortin estimates, based on the European Community example, that such an arrangement could impose *total* extra costs amounting to 0.6 percent of SQ's GDP (some $1 billion in 1991 dollars) annually; if so, the cost to ROC would probably be comparable in dollar terms, though obviously less by comparison with GDP. (Readers interested in the application of these principles in a different context — Canada's choice of maintaining a separate currency as opposed to using the U.S. dollar — will find the relevant analysis in Appendix B.)

Credibility Problems of a New Currency

Our earlier mention of the maintenance of the SQ currency's external value, however, draws attention to a major problem. Many Quebec-sized countries maintain separate currencies under adjustable-peg or even flexible-exchange-rate systems. But it is one thing for an already existing country to maintain the viability of an already existing currency and another thing entirely for a new country to create a new currency. A new currency can only establish itself as an economy-wide unit of account and means of exchange and a viable medium for use in international transactions if people voluntarily use it in these roles — or, to put it another way, if the currency becomes credible.

Supporters of Quebec independence even now lay great stress on the desirability of continued use of the Canadian dollar by a sovereign Quebec. This surely indicates their belief that Quebecers would be suspicious of a new SQ currency, and it suggests that the question of credibility is extremely important in this particular instance. If we are right about this, then it seems likely that, following an acrimonious breakup, Quebecers themselves — let alone those outside SQ — would be suspicious about the future stability of the purchasing power of a new currency. In other words, for those concerned about the value of their retirement savings, for example, the SQ currency's reliability as a standard of deferred payment would be in doubt.

Even if its launch were not accompanied — as it might well be — by large fluctuations in its value on foreign-exchange markets, the SQ currency in all likelihood would trade at a discount to its equilibrium value — that is, its purchasing/producing power parity value — as ordinary SQ residents, not to mention currency dealers, sought some "insurance" against the risks inherent in holding it. During the early years of the new currency's existence, real interest rates in SQ would probably be higher as well, as lenders demanded a premium for holding assets denominated in a riskier currency.[4] This discount would impose a cost on Quebecers in terms of their purchasing power in the rest of the world, and fluctuations in the exchange value of the new currency as a result of uncertainties about the economic policies of a new SQ government would increase that cost.

Problems for "the Rest of Canada"

A weak SQ currency would not just be a problem for SQ; it would also impose costs on ROC in terms of its competitive position. Since

---

4 It is often assumed that real interest rates in SQ (and ROC) would be higher over the long term as well, on the basis that smaller, less diversified economies — and the creditworthiness of their governments — are more vulnerable to external shocks. If this effect exists, however, comparisons across the countries of the Organisation for Economic Co-operation and Development over the past decade — the only period for which reasonably comparable interest rates are available for most countries — suggest that it is small. On average, smaller economies have tended to have higher real interest rates since 1979, but once the tendency of small economies to have current-account deficits — with an accompanying need to attract an offsetting capital inflow — during this period is allowed for, size of economy seems, in a statistical sense, to have little explanatory power as far as real interest rates are concerned.

1989, producers in Ontario, for example, have found themselves pressed to compete against the background of a Canada-U.S. exchange rate that has been, in inflation-adjusted terms, some 4½ percent above its average value over the previous two decades. They would find themselves in a very difficult position if their Quebec competitors, who already have well-established relationships with customers in the United States, not to mention in the rest of Canada, were to benefit from a comparable, or greater, cost advantage stemming from a weak SQ exchange rate. This raises the specter of other protectionist actions by ROC against SQ as well.

All of this would create a most unpleasant dilemma for ROC authorities. They could respond to the political pressures it would undoubtedly create by easing domestic monetary conditions, hence putting at risk several years of hard-won gains against inflation. Or they could be forced into cooperating with their counterparts in SQ in attempts to stabilize the value of the new currency, which would be particularly galling after an acrimonious breakup.

The issuing of a separate SQ currency would present other difficulties for ROC. It would have to cancel — possibly after they were collected by SQ authorities and presented by them for exchange into interest-bearing ROC debt or for ROC foreign-exchange reserves — up to one-quarter of outstanding Canadian dollar banknotes and coins, around $6.5 billion worth. Although this might occur over a long period, it would be the equivalent of 30 percent of the federal government's domestic financing requirement in the current fiscal year, or almost one-third of Canada's current foreign-exchange reserves. As a result, the ROC government would be deprived of seigniorage amounting to some 0.05 percent of GDP — about $360 million in 1991 dollars — annually over the next decade.

Redenominating Debt

The creation of the new currency would raise extra problems in connection with the already contentious matter of the division of existing federal government liabilities between ROC and SQ. Even if the division of debt obligations was speedily and amicably agreed on — an unlikely outcome[5] — there would now arise the additional question of what currency SQ's share would be denominated in. Would SQ continue to borrow abroad in (and pay interest in) ROC dollars, or would it attempt to market debt denominated in its own currency? If the latter, would the conversion be carried out all at once, or piecemeal as existing Canadian dollar debt matured? And, of course, related questions would arise not just with respect to currently existing federal debt, but to existing Canadian-dollar-denominated debt of the province of Quebec and such provincial agencies as Hydro-Québec.

The new SQ currency likely would be the object of more suspicion than the ROC dollar in foreign-exchange markets, at least initially. The SQ government, therefore, might be tempted to borrow in ROC dollars in order to reduce its interest costs. But doing so would impede the development of the SQ currency as a visible and credible one in foreign-exchange markets, thus perpetuating the problem. One need not predict how such an uncomfortable choice would be resolved in order to conclude that its very existence would only add to the unattractiveness of a new currency with a floating exchange rate as a solution to SQ's monetary arrangements.

A Pegged Exchange Rate for the SQ Currency

If the SQ government decided to issue its own new currency, individuals and businesses both inside and outside SQ would have to be persuaded to use and hold it in order for it to take on a stable and reliable value. At the same time the currency would have to be seen to have a stable and reliable value before they could be so persuaded. This, simply stated, is the essence of the credibility problem we have been discussing.

Particularly following an economically disruptive separation, an SQ government intent on issuing its own money would have to

---

5 See Thomas J. Courchene, *In Praise of Renewed Federalism*, The Canada Round 2 (Toronto: C.D. Howe Institute, 1991), pp. 25–29; and a forthcoming volume in the Canada Round series on the division of federal assets and debt by Daniel Desjardins et al.

break this vicious circle by offering a reliable guarantee of the currency's stability and reliability. And the guarantee would have to last long enough — perhaps a decade or more, though all such estimates must, in the nature of the case, be uninformed guesses — to enable the currency to establish its reputation. By far the most straightforward type of guarantee to offer would be a fixed exchange rate against either the ROC dollar or the U.S. dollar.

If considerations of reducing foreign-exchange risks for trade transactions dominated the choice, then the ROC dollar would be selected, because Quebec trades more extensively with other parts of Canada than with the United States. If matters of debt marketing were dominant, however, then the U.S. dollar would be more attractive because of its widespread use in international capital markets. Given that SQ would begin its existence heavily in debt, we suspect that the latter consideration would be more important and the U.S. dollar would be chosen, but very little in the following discussion hinges on this guess.

The Effects of Pegging on the Benefits of a Separate Currency

Except for short-run consequences flowing from the level at which the currency was pegged, a fixed exchange rate on either currency would make it impossible for SQ to choose its own long-run inflation rate. It would have to accept whatever inflation was compatible with the maintenance of the exchange rate. Similarly, the need to maintain a peg would, in some circumstances, circumscribe the SQ central bank's ability to defuse a domestic financial crisis by creating large amounts of SQ currency for the SQ banking system to hold. Nor, obviously, would exchange-rate changes be available to cushion the SQ economy against real shocks — although the way in which specific shocks impinged on the SQ economy would depend on whether the SQ currency was pegged to the U.S. or ROC dollar.

In short, if SQ opted for a separate currency whose credibility was ensured by a pegged exchange rate, it would necessarily forego most of the economic advantages of a separate currency while still encountering all the costs of computation and foreign-exchange transactions that accompany such an arrangement. Only if the creation of a separate currency had some sort of national symbolic importance for SQ would this option, in and of itself, be an attractive one. We are aware of no evidence to suggest that even Quebecers who favor sovereignty attach much value to such a symbol.

Pegging at the Wrong Level Would Hurt SQ and ROC

Desired or not, a separate SQ currency with a pegged exchange rate is nevertheless a distinct possibility and therefore requires more discussion. The first point to note is that to peg a new currency at an exchange rate that might have to be devalued would do nothing for the currency's credibility. Given uncertainty about the equilibrium value of a new SQ currency, not to mention a strong temptation for the SQ government to create competitive advantages for SQ producers in domestic and foreign markets, a new currency initially might well be pegged at a level lower than could be justified by a comparison of production costs in SQ and elsewhere.

An exchange rate pegged at such an artificially low level would be credible in the short run, since there would be little imminent prospect of devaluation. Even so, it would produce a situation unsustainable in the long run. Over time, pressure in SQ's current and/or capital account related to the undervalued currency, reinforced by efforts on the part of SQ wage earners to recover their lost purchasing power, would push SQ's real exchange rate up to its equilibrium level. If the nominal exchange rate remained fixed, this appreciation would take the form of rising prices and wages in SQ to the point where the initial competitive advantage had been eroded.

How long these effects would take to come through is hard to say. They could certainly be delayed by wage and price controls — and in the political climate that would accompany the creation of a new, sovereign state, these might be unusually effective. Sooner or later, however, SQ would experience domestic inflation that would create not only the usual economic and social costs, but would also imply the painful necessity of switching, in time, to a disinflationary policy stance to ensure that the pegged SQ currency did not begin to come under *downward* pressure. In the interim, however, a considerable amount of harm might be done to producers in ROC — not least in Ontario — who would find it hard indeed to compete with their SQ counterparts; and the longer SQ was able to contain its domestic inflation, the longer this "interim" would last.

Under these circumstances, the ROC authorities would face pressures akin to those that would arise under the flexible-exchange-rate scenario. They would not have the option of intervening to influence the value of a pegged SQ currency, but they would still face pressures to ease domestic monetary policy. If the SQ currency was pegged to the U.S. dollar, rather than to the ROC dollar, this easing could be accompanied by a competitive devaluation of the ROC dollar. This step, however, would bring problems of its own. It would generate inflationary pressures in ROC, and it might provoke further measures from SQ to regain its competitive edge. If the SQ currency was pegged to the ROC dollar, on the other hand, competitive devaluation would be ruled out, though ROC policies that might lead to the depreciation of both currencies against the U.S. dollar would not be. In either event, trouble with the United States — where domestic producers would not take kindly to the short-run consequences of such policies for their own competitive positions — would surely result.

This scenario is highly speculative, of course, but it points strongly to the conclusion that, from an economic standpoint, the creation of a separate SQ currency is as fraught with danger for ROC as it is for SQ.

Maintaining the Monetary Union

A central feature of the political division of Canada would be that SQ would not elect members to the ROC parliament, and would, therefore — barring further negotiations — not exercise the influence over ROC monetary policy that would stem from such representation. SQ might nonetheless choose to continue to use the ROC dollar while being completely unrepresented in policy formation for the monetary union.

Unilateral Use
of the ROC Dollar by SQ

An SQ government wishing to establish such a system would announce that it would accept only the ROC dollar in discharge of taxes, require that tax records and returns use the ROC dollar as the unit of account, and declare that the ROC dollar was legal tender in SQ. Such decrees would render the ROC dollar indistinguishable in many respects from the current Canadian dollar. Whether they would be sufficient in and of themselves to guarantee the viability of such a monetary regime is a point to which we return below, but for the moment let us assume that they would be.

To use the ROC dollar in this way would not affect SQ's control of its inflation rate relative to that which it could wield with a separate currency pegged to the ROC dollar. As already noted, it would have no long-run control over inflation under a pegged exchange rate, while the option of deploying domestic wage and price controls for shorter-run ends would still be available to it under a common currency. By unilaterally adopting the ROC dollar, SQ would give up some seigniorage — if nominal interest rates were around 10 percent, the first year's amount might be some $540 million. With lower inflation and lower interest rates, the average annual cost over the next decade might fall to some 0.21 percent of SQ's GDP (around $360 million in 1991 dollars).[6] Part of this burden would be manifested in the form of a persistent necessity to export

---

6 The Bélanger-Campeau Commission argues that SQ could be compensated for the seigniorage lost on the stock of currency in the hands of SQ inhabitants at the time of separation by excluding federal government debt held by the Bank of Canada at the time of independence from SQ's share of the federal debt — although such a solution would not free SQ from the burden of seigniorage...

additional goods and services (or borrow abroad) to the tune of 0.13 percent of GDP annually in exchange for the new currency to meet the required SQ economy's growing demand for money.[7] In return for this outlay, SQ would retain most of the benefits generated by the monetary union.

An arrangement like this might follow a friendly breakup, but it would be more likely to grow out of a more acrimonious parting. Not much ill feeling would be required for ROC to insist on remaining the sole owner of the ROC central bank; nor is it hard to envisage a refusal to permit SQ any representation in the Bank of ROC's decisionmaking — especially since, in pre-breakup negotiations, the Canadian federal government would have every strategic incentive to be uncooperative about future monetary arrangements between SQ and its ROC successor.

Difficulties for the ROC Central Bank

Refusal on the part of ROC to cooperate with SQ in its use of the ROC dollar would, however, impose costs on ROC. Although there are examples of one country using the currency of another — the Irish Free State's use of the pound sterling in the 1920s; Panama's current use of the U.S. dollar — these situations tend to involve countries that are very small relative to those whose currencies they are using. In the SQ-ROC case, however, use of the ROC dollar by an SQ whose

---

6 - cont'd.

...related to new currency emitted after separation (see Bélanger-Campeau Commission, *Report* [Quebec, March 27, 1991], p. 430). Realistically, however, this tradeoff seems more likely to present a bone of ill-tempered contention than a source of amicable agreement in negotiations over division of the debt, especially since it could only be justified if SQ's continued use of the ROC dollar were a certainty. As we argue below, uncertainty over the stability of this arrangement is likely to be a serious problem.

7 This export would not need to be directly to ROC, but could go through third countries that were earning ROC dollars by running their own trade surpluses with ROC.

economy would be about one-third the size of ROC's, but with different economic policies, financial regulations, and so on, would make the task of running monetary policy in ROC more difficult than it otherwise would be.

Whether the ultimate goal is price stability or some other objective, and whether the policy instruments chosen are interest rates or monetary aggregates, the interaction of the supply and demand for money is central to the operation of monetary policy. In the environment described here, however, roughly one-quarter of the demand for ROC dollars would emanate from SQ, and would be subject to SQ influences such as changes in the regulatory framework governing financial institutions operating in SQ. Furthermore, the smooth conduct of monetary policy is easier when the authorities have ready and immediate access to all manner of financial data. Within ROC they would have the power to collect those data, as the Bank of Canada now has within Canada, but not necessarily within SQ.

It is hard to say how serious the effects of all this would likely be. The SQ government would have no reason to disrupt the financial system deliberately, and many good reasons to help maintain its stability for the sake of their own citizens. Nor, at present, is the federal government's regulatory and data gathering authority absolute — substantial segments of the financial system are provincially regulated. (It is also worth noting that the widespread international use of U.S. dollars, completely beyond the purview of the U.S. Federal Reserve System, does not render the conduct of monetary policy in the United States impossible.) Nevertheless, a unilateral decision by SQ to continue to make use of the ROC dollar would make life more difficult for the ROC authorities — which, in turn, could create problems of confidence in the durability of the union.

ROC Realistically Cannot Prevent SQ from Using the ROC Dollar

For this or other reasons, the ROC authorities might be tempted to try to prevent SQ from using the ROC dollar. But an examination of the measures that would be necessary to do this reveals quickly that ROC would inflict on itself an unbearable cost.

As long as SQ residents wished to use bank deposits denominated in ROC dollars and as long as their own government encouraged them to do so, it would be profitable for bank offices in SQ to supply them. A decision by a short-sighted ROC government to legislate against ROC banks providing such a service through SQ branches or subsidiaries would reduce the profitability of the banks affected, but would not destroy the business. Any SQ-based bank or foreign-based bank with a branch in SQ that was able to acquire ROC dollars and short-term ROC-dollar-denominated securities would be able to accept ROC dollar deposits and make ROC-dollar-denominated loans in SQ. As long as ROC dollars and ROC-dollar-denominated securities continued to be traded freely on international markets, banks wishing to do ROC dollar business in SQ (or anywhere else) would have no difficulty obtaining the necessary assets to put such business on a sound basis.

For ROC to prevent this, it would have to eliminate the supply of ROC dollars to international markets though comprehensive controls — not just on transactions with SQ, but on *all* foreign-exchange transactions. Among other things, this would involve:

- the strict regulation of the export of ROC dollars — including those in the pockets of persons leaving the country;
- the imposition of foreign-exchange allowances for vacationers and business travelers;
- requirements that ROC residents hold only credit cards linked to ROC dollar lines of credit, and a prohibition on their use abroad;
- the introduction of controls on the acquisition of foreign exchange by importers, and of parallel requirements that all foreign exchange earned by exporters immediately be surrendered in exchange for ROC dollars; and
- the strict regulation of all foreign lending and borrowing by ROC firms, households, and governments — which obviously would have to be carried on solely in foreign currency (since

there would be no ROC dollars abroad to borrow) with interest payments being made in foreign currency obtainable only with official permits.

While there are elements of Canadian society among whom such controls might appear attractive as part of a comprehensive departure from a market economy, it seems extremely unlikely that most citizens would be willing to bear the costs which the imposition of such controls would create, or to tolerate such a massive intrusion of the state into their lives.

More on a Common Currency with Separate Financial Systems

ROC's grudging acceptance of SQ's use of its dollar would lead to a system where the two states would maintain separate financial systems. The most straightforward arrangement along these lines presumably would be two separately regulated sets of financial institutions and parallel clearing mechanisms, with some sort of arrangement for collecting cheques drawn in one jurisdiction and deposited in the other.

This would impose costs on Quebecers trading with ROC and vice versa. These costs would not have to be large relative to the volume of transactions to be onerous to those who would have to bear them. Total clearings though the Canadian Payments Association are currently 26 times greater than GDP and are growing more than twice as fast as GDP. Even if the additional costs involved amounted to only 1 percent *of 1 percent* of the value of all transactions across SQ's borders, the total might be close to $300 million annually.

But the implications of such a scenario go well beyond transactions costs. The Bank of Canada currently stands ready to act as lender of last resort to the Canadian financial system in the event of a financial crisis. Though it — or, more precisely, its successor institution, the Bank of ROC — would retain this responsibility *vis-à-vis* ROC, SQ would have to find some way of providing such facilities for its own financial system. It would have to create some entity well endowed with holdings of ROC dollars and highly marketable ROC dollar securities in order to play that role. However, since the entity in question would not have the same power to create ROC dollars as the ROC central bank, it could not offer the same degree of security to the SQ financial system.

The extent to which outside help to SQ would be available in the event of a domestic financial crisis presumably would depend on the extent to which ROC-based financial institutions maintained branches in SQ and the extent to which those branches were involved in the crisis. The Bank of ROC would find it very hard not to act as lender of last resort to any ROC bank that found itself in liquidity difficulties because of a run on its SQ branches; and the "too big to fail" doctrine might come into play in the event of solvency problems. With ROC and SQ operating different regulatory regimes under different legal systems, however, ROC financial institutions probably would prefer to conduct business in SQ through subsidiaries than through branches. The Bank of ROC would be under no obligation to act as lender of last resort to foreign subsidiaries of domestic banks.

Similar considerations arise with respect to the closely related matter of deposit insurance. At present, the Canada Deposit Insurance Corporation (CDIC) is in a position to act as a "backup" to the Quebec Deposit Insurance Board (QDIB), and the CDIC is itself backed up by the federal government — and hence, in fact, by the Bank of Canada — not to mention the Canadian taxpayer. Presumably, the QDIB would have to stand alone in the event that SQ came into being, even to the extent of insuring deposits in SQ subsidiaries, and perhaps even branches, of ROC-based institutions.

A Common Currency with a Common Financial System

In the light of the foregoing discussion, it would obviously be economically preferable for both SQ and ROC to keep the current financial system largely intact, with financial institutions in both states being subject to substantially similar regulatory systems and members of a common clearing system. SQ would have to agree that branches of banks headquartered elsewhere in Canada could continue to operate as before, on an equal footing with SQ financial institutions, and ROC would have to reciprocate.[8]

In the wake of a friendly parting, it is possible to imagine the preservation of a fully fledged monetary union in which the successor states use a common currency, participate in an integrated financial system, and share in the governance of the central bank. Since the Bank of Canada is a federal Crown corporation, it is conceivable that — as part of a general division of federal assets — its ownership could be divided between a majority holding vested in the government of ROC and a minority SQ interest. Old federal debt, jointly guaranteed by both ROC and SQ, would form, at least initially, the greatest part of a jointly governed central bank's assets.

Along with some guidelines on the distribution of profits, such an arrangement would ensure that a portion of the seigniorage earned by the joint central bank would be distributed to SQ. It would also make it legally straightforward to ensure some SQ representation in the bank's governance. The minority shareholder could be given the right to appoint a minority of members to the bank's board.[9] The Bank of ROC-SQ could remain as lender of last resort to the monetary union as a whole, and the (RO)CDIC could retain its present backup status *vis-à-vis* the (S)QDIB. Such an integrated

---

8 As John Chant has pointed out, however, this desirable outcome is not very likely, since even within the current federal framework, the federal government and Quebec have already taken approaches to the regulation of financial institutions that differ in significant ways. See John F. Chant, "Financial Regulation under Alternative Constitutional Arrangements" (Paper presented to a conference on "Economic Dimensions of Constitutional Change," Queen's University, John Deutsch Institute for the Study of Economic Policy, Kingston, Ont., June 4–6, 1991).

9 We do not believe that the current governance, or mandate, of the Bank of Canada is altogether satisfactory. It would be desirable to give the Bank a clear mandate to pursue price stability while strengthening the powers of a reconstituted board. See David E.W. Laidler, *How Shall We Govern the Governor? A Critique of the Governance of the Bank of Canada*, The Canada Round 1 (Toronto: C.D. Howe Institute, 1991).

arrangement would appear to require a common regulatory environment, presumably characterized by extensive grandfathering of existing provisions.

Continued Monetary
Union Benefits Both Sides

Of all the alternatives, maintenance of the monetary status quo is by far the most attractive from an economic point of view. Particularly in the absence of any symbolic importance for a separate currency, the advantages that SQ might gain from its own money seem to be far outweighed by the lower transactions costs and financial risks that would flow from the maintenance of the Canadian monetary union, with a joint ROC-SQ dollar as its currency.

Quebec currently exports over half of its output, and even though the Canadian common market is riddled with trade barriers, some 60 percent of those exports go to the rest of Canada. Quebec's financial system is also closely integrated with that of the rest of Canada: all major banks have extensive branch networks in Quebec; Quebec firms can and do raise capital, and Quebec savers can and do lend, throughout the Canadian monetary union without serious legal impediments. On the assumption that trade and capital mobility remain at least as free between SQ and ROC as they now are, the introduction of a separate SQ currency would introduce a whole array of computational and foreign-exchange transactions costs into trading arrangements without generating any offsetting benefits.

Just as it is in Quebec's economic interest to maintain the monetary status quo, so would it be in the economic interest of ROC to acquiesce in — indeed, actively to seek — this outcome. If trade in goods, services, and capital between SQ and ROC remained as free as it is now — which would likewise be in the best interests of both sides — the savings in transactions costs generated by a single currency would accrue to individuals and businesses on both sides of the new political border.

Chapter 4

The Political Dimension and the Dynamics of Breakup

The Complementarity of Economic and Monetary Union

The problem with the scenario described at the end of the previous chapter is that a common market, like a monetary system, will not run itself. It requires that property rights and contracts to exchange them be enforceable everywhere within its confines, and that health and safety regulations, licensing requirements, industrial policies, and government procurement practices not be used to subsidise or otherwise protect local producers. And in a common-market-mone-tary-union arrangement involving more than one political jurisdiction, in which many of the usual government policies to cushion sectors of their economies against various shocks are forbidden, it is also highly desirable to have market-wide labor mobility, not to mention the capacity to make fiscal transfers, to help with such problems. Coordinated fiscal policies are also highly desirable in such an arrangement.

This is why one market with one money is most likely to be an efficient and durable entity if it is presided over by one government vested with the powers to keep it so. Or, to put the same point in another way, if "the Rest of Canada" (ROC) and a sovereign Quebec (SQ) remained on such friendly terms that they could negotiate the preservation of the Canadian common market and monetary union as it now exists, it is hard to see why their friendship could not be extended to preserving some sort of political union as well.

The Likelihood of an
Acrimonious Breakup

Critically, however, this whole issue has arisen for the very reason that sufficient friendship to maintain the political union may be lacking. Accordingly, it is time to add to the previous technical discussion an assessment of the dynamics of breakup, to see how likely it is that an arrangement in the economic best interests of both parties might actually emerge.

Just because an outcome is technically viable and clearly desirable does not mean that political processes will deliver it; if matters were that simple, such things as wars, revolutions — even strikes — would never occur. As Tom Courchene has pointed out, an economic and monetary union between two partners of comparable but unequal size might be subject to economic and political stresses sufficiently strong to make it unstable.[1] Moreover, the very fact that the permanence of the monetary union could not be taken for granted might have consequences that would hasten its demise.

The Credibility of SQ's
Commitment to the Monetary Union

Negotiations between SQ and ROC over the division of federal assets and debt, as well as over the maintenance of a common market in goods and services, are likely to be acrimonious. It is hard to believe that, under those circumstances, ROC would display any more than grudging acceptance of a decision by SQ to use the ROC dollar as its currency or — even more unlikely — that ROC would go out of its way to make it easier for SQ to do so. Could an SQ government that truly desired to maintain the monetary union make a unilateral commitment to the ROC dollar that would be credible to depositors,

---

1 Thomas J. Courchene, *In Praise of Renewed Federalism*, The Canada Round 2 (Toronto: C.D. Howe Institute, 1991), pp. 44–59.

lenders, and investment professionals alike? If it could not, what might be the consequences of such skepticism?

As already discussed, markets would probably expect the value of a separate SQ currency, *if it were to be established*, to be set at a discount greater than could be justified by simple comparisons of production costs between SQ and ROC. SQ would, in the best of circumstances, come into existence heavily burdened with foreign debt, and the quality of that debt inevitably would be the object of some suspicion, even if the Canadian monetary union initially continued to exist. SQ would have an unusually high debt-to-GDP ratio for an independent nation, and would feel additional pressure from debt-service costs on its balance of payments to the extent that investors demanded higher interest rates on SQ debt than they do on Quebec's combined federal-provincial debt at present. Worse, SQ's trade balance would be exposed to cyclical swings that would no longer be compensated by fiscal transfers, and all this at the very time when SQ's access to export markets in both ROC and the United States was under negotiation.

Investors in SQ, ROC, and elsewhere would be conscious that such balance-of-payments pressures might push the SQ government into creating a separate currency and pegging it at a competitively low exchange rate. This is not likely to be — and we do not question the statements of Quebec sovereigntists on this point — the SQ government's preferred option: the costs of introducing a separate currency would be high and even within a monetary union, domestic wage and price controls could be used to engineer a lower real exchange rate for SQ. But the mere existence of the possibility might well create a vicious circle.

Investors — whether private savers or pension fund managers — with doubts about the strength of SQ's commitment to the use of the ROC dollar would be bound to regard any assets held within SQ as being subject to the risk of redenomination into an undervalued SQ currency and perhaps the imposition of exchange controls, and might begin to pull capital out of SQ. And, importantly, if such a capital flight seemed remotely possible, even those utterly convinced of the sincerity of the SQ government's good intentions on the monetary front might begin to doubt its capacity to live up to those intentions, and move their money anyway. In this case, the desirability of the ROC dollar as a standard of deferred payment in SQ would be in doubt. The result would be a contraction of money and credit in SQ, possibly exacerbated by a run from bank deposits into currency, and, in short order, downward pressure on SQ output and incomes.

Under these circumstances, the advantages of a separate currency for dealing with a financial crisis would become increasingly attractive to the SQ government. The introduction, and rapid injection, of a new currency would permit any liquidity crisis in the banking system to be relieved. A devaluation, accompanied by (temporary) capital controls, might slow or halt the flight of capital. Besides, the weakness of the ROC dollar and the upward pressure on ROC interest rates that would accompany the crisis would make abandoning the ROC dollar appear less costly. And, as investors realized that the incentives facing the SQ government were shifting in favor of a new currency, the crisis of confidence would be exacerbated, likely hastening the very event they feared.

To summarize, then, universal confidence in the good intentions of the SQ government *vis-à-vis* monetary arrangements would be self-reinforcing. If everyone shared our faith in those intentions, SQ's ability unilaterally to maintain the existence of a Canadian monetary union, even after an acrimonious separation, would be enhanced. With confidence anything less than universal, the interaction of expectations and outcome could instead be destabilizing. Even if everyone did share our faith in the good intentions of SQ, *but erroneously believed that others did not*, that erroneous belief, widely enough held, would undermine attempts by SQ unilaterally to maintain its commitment to a monetary union with ROC.

We confess that we do not know how seriously to take this unpleasant scenario, any more than we know how seriously to take the possibility of a mutually destructive cycle of devaluation and inflation in SQ and ROC should the former opt for, or — as we now must also say — be forced to opt for, a separate currency. We cannot, however, rule out the possibility that SQ might be forced by markets to create its own currency. Our decision to end the title of this essay with a question mark was not gratuitous, but carefully calculated.

Concluding Comment

The implications of this essay are easily summarized, and their moral is easily drawn. The economic benefits that currently accrue from the existence of a common Canadian market, even the present imperfect one, and from the Canadian monetary union that goes with it, are large and worth preserving. Their loss would be serious, not only for Quebec, but for all of Canada. They provide a strong economic foundation to the case for maintaining Canada as a political federation.

If that case does not carry the day, and the political federation disintegrates, a straightforward economic analysis suggests that the benefits of a continued monetary union are still there to be preserved. From the point of view of both ROC and SQ, the economic desirability of the various options considered here can be ranked as follows: first, continued use of the ROC dollar by SQ with a joint central bank; second, continued use of the ROC dollar by SQ without SQ participation in the ROC central bank; third, a separate SQ currency with a pegged exchange rate; and last, a separate SQ currency with a flexible exchange rate.

This appears to be well understood in Quebec, where few now show much inclination to disrupt this aspect of the economic status quo — although the actual outcome of an acrimonious breakup where nationalist feelings are running high may be quite different. It needs to be equally well understood in other parts of Canada that much would be lost from the destruction of the monetary union. And it also needs to be understood that it is not within the power of ROC to disrupt the union with a view to punishing SQ without inflicting considerable damage on itself.

Critically, however, the strong economic case for preserving the Canadian economic union, including its monetary aspects, and the congruence of the interests of Quebec and other parts of Canada in this respect, is no guarantee that the monetary union would survive Quebec's secession. Forces inherent in the uncertain political dynamics of separation conceivably could undermine the continued existence of a monetary union — even a monetary union that everyone desired — to the considerable economic cost of all Canadians.

Appendix A

Data Sources and Calculations

Transactions Costs of Separate Currencies

The costs imposed by conducting business in more than one currency are manifold, and some of them are hard to identify. Nevertheless, it is possible to guess at magnitudes in some cases.

As far as the costs of currency conversion are concerned, the highly competitive nature of the foreign-exchange market suggests that spreads between wholesale (interbank) bid and ask rates ought to be reasonable guides to the resource cost of converting one currency to another and back again. If this is so, the cost of a straight conversion ought to be one half of the interbank bid/ask spread. Multiplying the relevant percentage by the appropriate volume of transactions, therefore, seems a good estimate of the cost of conducting business between two currencies.

The Case of Canada's Potential Use of the U.S. Dollar

In the case of Canadian-U.S. dollar business (see Appendix B for a complete discussion of the arguments for and against Canada's maintenance of a separate currency), some relevant figures are available. Kevin Clinton's 1988 study calculates half of the average bid/ask spread on spot transactions between the two currencies at 0.028 percent, with the comparable figure for swap and forward transactions being 0.054 percent.[1] The Bank of Canada's April 1989 survey of the Canadian foreign-exchange market shows transactions of US$195 billion during the month, with spot and forward/swap transactions accounting for 30 and 70 percent of the total respectively.[2] With perhaps two-thirds as much trading again taking place in U.S. and U.K. markets,[3] total Canadian-U.S. dollar trading may have amounted to around $4.8 trillion at an annual rate — equal to more than 21 times Canada-U.S. trade in goods and services.

Weighting the costs of the two types of trades and multiplying by the total amount of trading suggests that the annual cost of Canadian-U.S. dollar conversions was at that time of the order of $2.2 billion. If half of this was borne by Canadians, the cost would amount to about 0.17 percent of GDP, or $1.2 billion in 1991 dollars.

The European Community's estimates of the costs of separate currencies are more comprehensive, attempting to incorporate corporate in-house bookkeeping costs, and so on.[4] Inasmuch as these estimates are a function of openness of the individual countries to trade, and since intra-EC merchandise trade amounted to some 27 percent of the EC's GDP in 1988 — roughly similar to Canada's merchandise trade with the United States (30 percent of Canadian GDP) — the Community's estimate of a total cost of 0.4 percent of GDP for the EC as a whole may be applicable to Canada.

The Case of SQ's Use of the ROC Dollar

Converting numbers like this into something applicable to the situation of a separate SQ currency involves a number of necessarily very rough guesses.

---

1 Kevin Clinton, "Transactions Costs and Covered Interest Arbitrage: Theory and Evidence," *Journal of Political Economy* 96 (1988): 363.

2 Cindy Sawchuk and George Pickering, "Survey of the Canadian Foreign Exchange Market," *Bank of Canada Review* (October 1989), p. 7.

3 Ibid., p. 15.

4 Commission of the European Communities, Directorate General for Economic and Financial Affairs, "One Market, One Money," *European Economy* 44 (October 1990), Annex A.

First of all, one set of figures submitted to the Bélanger-Campeau Commission shows Quebec's trade in goods and services with the rest of Canada to be equal to about 65 percent of Quebec's GDP (15 percent of Canada's GDP).[5] If the ratio of SQ-ROC foreign-exchange transactions to SQ-ROC trade were equal to the ratio of Canadian-U.S. dollar transactions to Canada-U.S. trade (21 times), they would amount to some 3.2 times combined ROC-SQ GDP. If this number is reliable, an estimate of the bottom end of potential transaction costs in SQ-ROC dollar trading can be obtained by assuming (somewhat unrealistically) that bid/ask spreads on this business would be no larger than those on Canadian-U.S. dollar trades. This calculation yields a transaction cost of 0.14 percent of combined ROC-SQ GDP — or some $1 billion in 1991 dollars, of which half presumably would be borne by SQ.

Bernard Fortin modifies the EC figures based on Quebec's greater openness to trade and arrives at a figure of 0.6 percent of SQ's GDP for total transaction costs — or about $1 billion in 1991 dollars. If this estimate is correct, ROC presumably would bear a comparable cost in dollar terms — although as a proportion of ROC's GDP it would be of the order of 0.2 percent.

Seigniorage

The concept of "seigniorage", while unfamiliar to most people, is important enough to this discussion to be worth exploring in some detail. In this section, we explain how seigniorage arises and show

---

5 Pierre-Paul Proulx and Guilan Cauchy, "Un examen des échanges commerciaux du Québec avec les autres provinces canadiennes, les États-Unis et le reste du monde," in Quebec, Commission on the Political and Constitutional Future of Quebec [Bélanger-Campeau Commission], *Éléments d'analyse économique pertinents à la révision du statut politique et constitutionnel du Québec* [Background papers], vol. 1 (Quebec, 1991), pp. 140, 154, 157. Another set of figures on Quebec's trade with the rest of Canada in goods alone is available in Patrice Muller and Shane Williamson, "Economic Linkages Among Provinces," *Quarterly Economic Review* (Department of Finance), March 1991, p. 52. Generally speaking, data on interprovincial trade are weak and need to be treated with caution.

how it can be calculated in Canada's current circumstances. We then go on to provide some rough calculations relevant to the scenarios of (a) an independent Quebec and (b) Canada's use of the U.S. dollar.

What Is Seigniorage?

The term seigniorage itself harks back to earlier times, when money consisted mainly of gold and silver coins, the minting of which was often a local feudal monopoly. Individuals bringing bullion to the mint to be turned into coin would receive in return coin whose metallic content was a little less than the bullion they supplied. This surplus metal accrued to the lord — the "seigneur" — who held the monopoly over the mint. It represented a fee for the mint's services. Being available to be turned into coin that could be used to defray the seigneur's expenses, "seigneurage" (or seigniorage) was often an important source of his revenue.

Nowadays, seigniorage refers to the return that accrues to the monetary authorities — the national government and the central bank — from the ability to issue currency. Currency is a liability of the monetary authorities, but, unlike other government financial liabilities, it bears no interest. The individuals and businesses who hold it are foregoing the income they could receive by holding, say, treasury bills instead.

Calculating Seigniorage

In Canada's case, when new paper money created by the Bank of Canada and new coins created by the Royal Canadian Mint enter circulation, they allow the federal government — to which the profits of both institutions are remitted — to obtain goods and services in exchange for a non-interest-bearing liability (rather than by issuing bonds or treasury bills). During a given period of time, the interest not paid by the government as a result of the existence of these liabilities, net of the expense of maintaining them such as reprinting notes, represents its seigniorage.

With respect to paper money outstanding, the Bank of Canada's financial statements offer a convenient way of estimating this saving. At year-end 1990, the Bank of Canada had some $24.8 billion of non-interest-bearing liabilities outstanding, most of which was currency.[6] On the asset side of its balance sheet, it had some $24.7 billion in interest-bearing federal government debt. The difference between the Bank's revenue — that is, interest income — and expenses in 1990 amounted to $2.4 billion. This amount was remitted to the federal government, making the bulk of the federal government's debt held by the Bank effectively interest-free. This represents the greatest part of the Canadian monetary authorities' seigniorage in 1990.

The calculation with respect to coins is more difficult, since the Mint does not hold interest-bearing assets against currency outstanding, but simply remits profits to the federal government, reducing the government's need to issue interest-bearing debt. However, logic similar to that of the Bank of Canada calculation — a dollar's worth of coin is initially more expensive to produce than a dollar's worth of paper money, but lasts virtually indefinitely — allows one to estimate a rough figure. Outstanding coins intended for circulation — as opposed to commemoratives and the like — at year-end 1990 amounted to $2.2 billion. If the ratio of net interest saved to non-interest-bearing liabilities applicable to the Mint is comparable to that of the Bank, seigniorage from this source would have amounted to a little over $0.2 billion in 1990.

This method of calculation suggests that total seigniorage arising from the Canadian monetary authorities' operations in 1990 was about $2.6 billion, or 0.39 percent of GDP.[7]

---

6 In addition to currency, the Bank's non-interest-bearing liabilities also consist of cheques outstanding (a very small amount), federal government deposits, and deposits of chartered banks and other members of the Canadian Payments Association. Although this latter item, much of which reflects the reserves chartered banks are required to hold against their deposit liabilities, is currently quite large (some $1.6 billion at the end of 1990), its importance will diminish as Canada moves to a zero-reserve system. Accordingly, this discussion focuses primarily on currency, and calculations are made with respect to currency only.

7 Another method of estimating seigniorage is to focus on the emission of new liabilities — by which the monetary authorities purchase goods and services...

Growth of seigniorage over time is sensitive to growth in the economy, which tends to increase the demand for currency, although by a less-than-proportionate amount; to increases in the price level, which tend to raise demand for currency on a one-for-one basis; and to interest rates, which have the partially offsetting effects of raising the value of the government's interest saving, but simultaneously reducing demand for currency.[8] Calculating it prospectively, therefore, involves estimating how much currency will be outstanding and multiplying it by the expected nominal interest rate. The first of these quantities is a function of real economic growth (the elasticity of demand for currency with respect to growth of real incomes is assumed to be 0.7), inflation (the elasticity of demand for currency with respect to the price level is assumed to be 1.0), and interest rates (the elasticity of demand for currency with respect to interest rates is assumed to be -0.278);[9] the second is a function of the real interest rate and inflation.

---

7 - *cont'd.*

from the private sector in return for an essentially costless product — in a given period of time. This approach typically will give a different result for seigniorage in a given period, mainly because it overlooks the real interest currently being saved on money issued in the past. (Moreover, the Bank of Canada's net emission of non-interest-bearing liabilities was very small in 1990, in keeping with its non-inflationary stance and the reduced demand for new money from an economy in recession.)

8 Since the latter effect becomes more important as nominal interest rates rise, and since nominal interest rates rise with the rate of inflation — which, in turn, depends on the rate of money creation — there is an upper limit to the revenue that the authorities can raise from seigniorage. A formal analysis of these issues is presented in David E.W. Laidler, "Monetary Expansion and the Revenue of the Monetary Authority: A Geometric Exposition," in Michael Artis and A. Robert Nobay, eds., *Essays in Economic Analysis: Proceedings of the Association of University Teachers of Economics Annual Conference, Sheffield 1975* (Cambridge: Cambridge University Press, 1976).

9 The elasticities of currency demand are from Francesco Caramazza, Kim McPhail, and Doug Hostland, "Studies on the Demand for M2 and M2+ in Canada" (Paper presented at the Bank of Canada monetary seminar, Ottawa, May 8, 1990), p. 47.

The Case of SQ's Potential Use of the ROC Dollar

Using the above elasticities and assumptions of 3.4 percent average GDP growth, 1.5 percent inflation, and 4.3 percent average real interest rates over the decade from 1992 to 2001 yields total Bank of Canada seigniorage over the next ten years averaging 0.21 percent of GDP ($1.5 billion in 1991 dollars).[10] If these assumptions held following Quebec independence, SQ's seigniorage cost of using the ROC dollar would amount to roughly one-quarter of this amount: around $360 million.

If the Bank of Canada abandons its pursuit of price stability and inflation is, say, 6 percent over the next decade, the parameters used here suggest that seigniorage would amount to some 0.35 percent of GDP on average — a little over $2.4 billion in 1991 dollars. This would raise the seigniorage cost to SQ of using the ROC dollar to an average of around $600 million (1991 dollars) annually.

The Case of Canada's Potential Use of the U.S. Dollar

Calculating the seigniorage cost to Canada of using the U.S. dollar involves using the same parameters, but modifying the economic assumptions to reflect the new arrangement. The figures presented in Appendix B assume an average U.S. inflation rate of 4 percent and an average real interest rate of 3.5 percent from 1992 to 2001, which yields an average annual seigniorage cost of 0.26 percent of GDP — or $1.8 billion in 1991 dollars. To the extent that U.S. inflation was higher, the seigniorage cost to Canada would rise as well: at a 6 percent average inflation rate, annual seigniorage would amount to 0.33 percent of GDP on average — or $2.3 billion in 1991 dollars.

---

10 This amount is smaller than 1990's 0.39 percent of GDP because it is assumed that inflation and nominal interest rates will decline over the decade.

The Size of the Economy and the Variability of Real Exchange Rates

As noted, the importance of nominal exchange-rate movements in easing adjustments to real shocks depends on the speed with which domestic prices and costs respond to changes in market conditions and/or the exchange rate, which, in turn, is likely to be largely a function of the size and openness of the economy in question.

A rough guide to this relationship is available in the real effective exchange rates based on value-added deflators in manufacturing calculated by the International Monetary Fund. These indexes measure the degree to which factor costs in a given country are out of line with the nominal exchange rate against trading partners. Barring a persistent positive relationship between the size of a country's economy and its susceptibility to real shocks — which seems unlikely, unless large capital markets increase this susceptibility — their variability over time ranked against size of economy seems a plausible indicator of the degree to which economic size allows discrepancies between domestic and foreign factor prices to persist, and hence of the ability of nominal exchange-rate changes to ease the adjustment to real shocks.

The figure on the opposite page shows the results of a regression of the average absolute two-year change in the real effective exchange rates of 15 countries against the size of their economies from 1975 to 1989. The implied relationship indicates that factor-price discrepancies persist about one-third longer in Canada-sized economies than in Quebec-sized economies.

The Costs of a Divided Clearing System

In the absence of a clear idea of what a divided ROC-SQ clearing system might look like, it is impossible to come up with any solid figures on the costs that it would impose. It is nevertheless worth pointing out the phenomenal size of the clearing system in Canada:

**Real Effective Exchange-Rate Variability
as a Function of Economic Size**

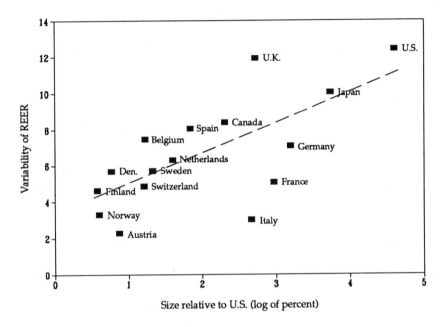

Note: Variability is the average absolute two-year percentage change in the real
effective exchange rate over the 1975–89 period.
Source: International Monetary Fund, *International Financial Statistics Yearbook*
(Washington, D.C., 1990).

the total value of transactions processed through the Canadian
Payments Association amounted to $17.44 trillion in 1990 — 26 times
1990 GDP. As an upper limit to the fraction that might be attributable
to Quebec/rest-of-Canada transactions, it seems plausible to use the
ratio of Quebec/rest-of-Canada trade to Canadian GDP: 15 percent.
This would put the value of such clearings at just less than 4 times
GDP, or $2.71 trillion in 1991 dollars; 1 percent of 1 percent of this
amount is $270 million.

Appendix B

Should Canada Have Its Own Dollar?

The maintenance of a separate national currency in general involves both costs and benefits. In the SQ-ROC case, the relevant calculus points strongly in the direction of SQ's continuing to use the ROC dollar as its currency even in the event of Canada's political breakup.

What about monetary relations between Canada and the United States, then? Canada, which is much smaller relative to the United States than SQ would be relative to ROC — Canada's economy is about 10 percent as large as that of the United States; SQ's economy would be about 30 percent as large as ROC's — at present maintains a separate currency, with a flexible exchange rate into the bargain, despite a large volume of trade with the United States and a high degree of capital mobility between the two countries. Would a dispassionate deployment of the analysis in this essay to the Canada-U.S. case lead to the conclusion that the use of the U.S. dollar throughout North America is desirable? In this Appendix, we argue that the cost-benefit calculus works out differently in the Canada-U.S. case and that current arrangements probably are preferable to the adoption by Canada of the U.S. dollar as its currency.

Eliminating Transactions Costs between the Canadian and U.S. Dollars

In Canada's case, the savings from adopting the currency of its largest trading partner would be considerable. Calculation and transactions costs, as well as exchange-rate risk, would be eliminated for at least 70 percent of Canada's external trade, and for a sizable proportion of its capital transactions as well. Financial transactions costs amounting to perhaps 0.17 percent of GDP — $1.2 billion in 1991 dollars — might be eliminated in such a step (see Appendix A). If the European Community's research on the costs associated with the EC's separate currencies is applicable to Canada, the total saving might to as much as 0.4 percent of GDP — or about $2.8 billion. Against this benefit — and setting aside the symbolic implications of such a move — Canada would be exposed to significant potential costs in each area mentioned in this paper.

Accepting the U.S. Inflation Rate

As far as the rate of inflation is concerned, the Bank of Canada's commitment to price stability, amply demonstrated by its disinflationary stance of the past three years, has now been reinforced by a series of inflation targets that point to the eradication of inflation by the second half of the 1990s. Despite occasional public pronouncements, the current commitment of the U.S. Federal Reserve to price stability is less clear. The shaky state of the U.S. financial system and the fact that the United States' considerable — and growing — external liabilities are denominated in U.S. dollars are two factors giving a potential inflationary bias to future U.S. monetary policy. In contrast to the experience of most of the postwar period, the next decade may well be one in which Canada's inflation performance is consistently better than that of the United States.

Although empirical evidence on this point is mixed, some studies have estimated the damage to the Canadian economy from inflation to be very large.[1] By choosing the U.S. dollar as its money, Canada might also end up choosing a higher inflation rate — with

---

1 Farid Novin (*The Productivity-Inflation Nexus Revisited: Canada, 1969–88*, Working Paper 91-1 [Ottawa: Bank of Canada, 1991]) estimates that every 1 percentage point increase in inflation lowers total factor productivity growth by 0.3 percent. Assuming that inflation affects the productivity of capital only, and only the level, not the growth rate, the discounted value of the gain resulting from 1 percent lower inflation is still larger than current GDP. See Peter Howitt, "Zero Inflation as a Long-Term Target for Monetary Policy," in Richard G. Lipsey, ed., *Zero Inflation: The Goal of Price Stability* (Toronto: C.D. Howe Institute, 1990), p. 106.

the attendant economic damage and social stress — than it could achieve on its own by maintaining a separate currency.

Loss of Seigniorage

In addition, Canada's use of the U.S. dollar would involve costs in lost seigniorage. The Canadian government would have to pay interest on that fraction of its debt currently represented by the non-interest-bearing liabilities of the Bank of Canada. As explained in Appendix A, some fairly standard assumptions about interest rates and economic growth suggest that, were Canada to adopt the U.S. dollar, the average annual seigniorage cost might amount to some 0.26 percent of GDP — about $1.8 billion in 1991 dollars — over the next decade. Part of this cost would appear as a need on Canada's part to export additional goods and services (or borrow abroad) an amount equivalent to some 0.22 percent of GDP annually in exchange for new U.S. currency. Interest foregone on this amount would add to the next and subsequent years' seigniorage costs.

Loss of the Bank of Canada as Lender of Last Resort

Canada would also lose the services of the Bank of Canada as lender of last resort to the Canadian financial system. The Bank currently stands prepared to provide liquidity to the directly clearing members of the Canadian Payments Association and to provide extended last resort loans to chartered banks; it also ultimately — though informally, through the federal government — stands behind the Canada Deposit Insurance Corporation, which can also act as lender of last resort for its members. Unless Canada's banks and near-banks were integrated into the U.S. Federal Reserve and Federal Deposit Insurance systems, with all the legal and regulatory changes involved, Canada would need to form a new monetary authority with a war chest of U.S. dollars large enough to prevent the failure of a large financial institution in the event of a run on its deposits.

Greater Vulnerability to External Shocks

As far as coping with external shocks is concerned, Canada also appears to be well served by a separate currency. First of all, the United States and Canada have sufficiently different economic structures that external shocks often affect them in markedly different ways — a change in the world price of oil being a ready example. Second, the Canadian economy is large enough that the reaction of nominal domestic prices and costs to changes in the exchange rate tends to be incomplete, even after a period of years. Under these circumstances, the ability of a flexible exchange rate to cushion output and employment in the Canadian economy from external shocks is high.

The Credibility of the Canadian Dollar

Perhaps the biggest difference between the SQ-ROC scenario and the Canada-U.S. case lies in the fact that the Canadian dollar is an already existing currency with considerable credibility. Many of the disadvantages — and potentially the most severe — that would arise from SQ's trying to establish its own currency would stem from its newness. These disadvantages, which argue strongly against a separate SQ currency, simply do not exist for the already well established Canadian dollar, and are therefore irrelevant to arguments about the desirability of its continued existence.

For all these reasons, then, the cost-benefit calculus seems to work out in favor of maintaining the Canadian dollar separate from its U.S. counterpart.[2]

---

2 Note that, if the case for maintaining a separate Canadian dollar is favorable, the case for maintaining a floating exchange rate is even more so. As already discussed in the SQ context, a pegged exchange rate would deprive Canada of the benefits of choosing its own inflation rate and cushioning its economy from external shocks, but would still involve numerous transactions costs and — at least for the first few years of a peg — some exchange-rate risk as well. See David E.W. Laidler and William B.P. Robson, *The Fix Is Out: A Defense of the Floating Canadian Dollar*, C.D. Howe Institute Commentary 18 (Toronto: C.D. Howe Institute, 1990).

A Comment

Lloyd C. Atkinson

David Laidler and Bill Robson have provided an excellent taxonomic assessment of the alternative currency and monetary arrangements that could prevail in the event that Quebec assumes the status of a sovereign state. The separation of Quebec from Canada would be costly — both to the sovereign Quebec (SQ) *and* to "the Rest of Canada" (ROC). And the costs could be enlarged — potentially significantly — depending on the monetary arrangements adopted, and/or agreed to, by both SQ and ROC. In this regard, it is difficult to find fault with Laidler's and Robson's conclusions. However, to expand the discussion modestly, three additional considerations should be given emphasis.

First, I think it would be a mistake to underestimate the negative consequences for Canada's financial markets of a breakup of Canada into two (or more) nations. It is difficult to imagine that such a breakup, if it were to occur, could be anything other than acrimonious no matter what kind of face each side tried to put on it. The question of which government would accept responsibility for the debt contracted earlier in the name of Canada, or Quebec, or some other province, would weigh heavily on the minds of both foreign *and* domestic creditors. The inevitable question on the mind of the foreign investor would be: "Do I really want to play in the traffic while Canadians sort out these matters? Would it not be better to park, temporarily at least, my investments elsewhere?" Parking those investments elsewhere — implying, of course, the sell-off of Canadian dollar assets — could precipitate a major Canadian dollar crisis. Canada's net external debt is huge — close to $250 billion; the

Bank of Canada's stabilization fund is much smaller — currently close to $17 billion.

But it is not just our external creditors we would need to worry about: if external creditors can be spooked, so can asset holders resident in Canada. Moreover, it is worth remembering that it would require only a fractional unloading of Canadian-dollar assets by external creditors (not to mention resident creditors) to precipitate a currency crisis with all of its attendant negatives (for example, higher real rates of interest, slower growth, higher unemployment). Prices are, after all, set at the margin.

Such a currency crisis would count as a "breakup" cost. It is the costs over and above this and other "breakup" costs that are the subject of Laidler's and Robson's analysis. By comparison with these "breakup" costs — and depending on whether or not the "breakup" costs were short-lived — the added costs associated with the monetary arrangements agreed to could be of secondary importance.

There is a second consideration: while I agree with Laidler and Robson that the maintenance of a monetary union would be the least risky and least costly of the alternative monetary arrangements, I have serious doubts that such an arrangement constitutes a workable alternative. Laidler and Robson acknowledge that "the political and confidence-related dynamics of an acrimonious separation" could indeed make this arrangement unworkable. But a practical consideration could undermine the monetary union arrangement even in the unlikely event of an amicable parting of the ways: given all of the considerations that led to the breakup in the first place, can one imagine an SQ willing to cede to ROC complete[1] sovereignty over something as important as monetary policy — all the more so if the financial-market outcome of the breakup of the country re-

---

1 The word "complete" is used advisedly. The currency of choice in a monetary union would be the ROC dollar; the central bank would be the "Bank of ROC". A sharing of powers, in the sense of providing Quebec veto authority over "Bank of ROC" policies, would likely seriously undermine international confidence in the ROC dollar, unless such veto power were used exclusively to counter an inflationary ROC monetary policy.

sulted in a heavily indebted Quebec having to endure punishingly high interest rates?

A final consideration: while Laidler and Robson limit their discussion to the monetary arrangements between SQ and ROC, it is not at all apparent that a union of the nine remaining provinces would occur in the event of Quebec sovereignty. How would ROC deal with the fact that, by population and output, Ontario would carry a weight in excess of 50 percent? And how would current federally administered transfer programs be kept intact in an environment where zero-basing everything would be high on everyone's agenda? Bluntly put, while Quebec may not be the cement that holds us all together, its separation would be the wedge that drives us all apart.

These considerations lead me to the conclusion that the establishment of an independent Quebec would result in the creation of a separate Quebec currency — risky though that outcome would be. Its rate of exchange could be flexible or fixed, and if fixed it might — for practical reasons — have to be fixed to the U.S. dollar, because it is not apparent that there would remain a ROC and, therefore, a ROC dollar to which it could be fixed.

A Comment

John Grant

Monetary matters are not central to the constitutional struggles of the 1990s. But a separate Quebec, if it came to that, would have to make its choice of currency, and "the Rest of Canada" (ROC) would have to respond. Somewhat coincidentally, informed thinking in Canada on the subject of central banking seems to have advanced to the point where rewording of the *Bank of Canada Act* is, in any case, in order; so we should make use of this opportunity to devise something better, not worse, than what we have at present.

A separate Quebec would have to deal with two issues in this area: first, choosing a currency and, second, deciding how to regulate its deposit-taking financial institutions. Quebec's economy is very open, both to the rest of Canada and to the United States, and there would be a case for its adopting either the Canadian or the U.S. dollar as its currency. (One could also imagine a third case, a kind of *laissez-faire* outcome, in which Quebec would declare both the Canadian and the U.S. dollars to be legal tender, leaving to its citizens the day-to-day decision as to the volume of cash balances they wished to hold in each currency for purposes of making payments or as a store of value. But I do not expect to see it.)

Although a separate Quebec could create a distinct currency of its own, concerns of credibility and convenience would require a fixed exchange rate with one dollar or the other. Even then, lenders would certainly price some risk of devaluation into interest rates, leading Quebecers and others to avoid its use where possible. Many Quebecers would probably choose to hold only minimal transactions balances in that form and would keep the bulk of their monetary wealth denominated in other currencies. Having thus

sensibly decided to avoid creating its own currency, Quebec would
have essentially two choices: to become one-third of the First Federal
Reserve District, under the aegis of the Federal Reserve Bank of
Boston, or to remain one-quarter of the Canadian monetary area,
under the supervision of the Bank of Canada. (These proportions
reflect the size of Quebec's economy.)

Since the acrimony associated with separation undoubtedly
would be severe — given, for example, the difficulty of apportioning
national assets and liabilities — it is possible that ROC might not
look favorably on accepting formal membership by Quebec in its
monetary area. However, I find this very unlikely: it would be stupid
in the extreme for ROC to reject Quebec, an important trading
partner, a co-guarantor of a healthy chunk of the financial assets and
liabilities owned and owed by ROC, and a potentially important
payer of seigniorage to the Canadian central bank. Mutual dislike
would probably not prevent ROC from accepting a junior partner
whose power to disturb its rest would be reduced, not enhanced, by
doing so.

As far as choosing the First Federal Reserve District is concerned — assuming that the United States was interested in expand-
ing it — the problem here would be the practical one that Quebec's
banks are all thoroughly and deeply linked to ROC. Forcing them to
break apart, so that the Quebec parts would report to the Fed while
the remainder reported to Canada, would be a great and costly
perversity. Given the domination of Quebec's financial structure by
the Canadian chartered banks, this really is not much of a choice.

A separate Quebec would find itself obliged to regulate banks
and banking. But as part of a Canadian monetary union, the new
state would have little freedom in these matters. Attempts to increase
taxation of deposit interest — or, for that matter, bank capital —
beyond the rates applied in ROC would quickly spur the flight of
deposits to branches outside Quebec's borders. In any case, bank
regulation in the 1990s is becoming increasingly harmonized inter-
nationally. The rules governing ownership and control of financial
institutions represent one area in which Quebec and Canada have

maintained important differences, which Quebec might propose to extend to banking. But if Quebec wished to encourage greater foreign ownership of the banking sector, it would still find this exceedingly difficult to achieve if ROC, the dominant domicile for the Schedule A banks, were to oppose it.

Central banking is one of the most sophisticated inventions of the past 70 years. Although the Bank of England was established as long ago as 1694 and many of the essential regulatory functions of a central bank were developed during the nineteenth century, it was not until the 1920s that the U.S. Federal Reserve System began to become aware, in the modern sense, of its responsibility for carrying out macroeconomic policy. Only recently, in assessing the worldwide inflation cycle just ending, have central banks finally recognized clearly what they can and cannot do. With reasonable luck, they can pretty reliably determine the three-to-five-year trend of inflation, and with some help from their colleagues, they can moderate excessive day-to-day swings in exchange rates. But almost everything else they have been asked to do involves trickery of some sort, which, when it is inevitably found out, generally worsens the record it was meant to improve. In particular, efforts to reduce unemployment by reducing interest rates — the nostrum still beloved by politicians who are not in positions of responsibility — are bound to fail, and regularly have failed, despite the most elaborate stratagems. So central bankers and their political masters in major industrial countries appear to have decided to aim monetary policy on the whole at achieving a very low, or zero, inflation rate in the medium term, having finally — and, I would say, correctly — despaired of doing better.

Whether or not Quebec separates, it appears that the *Bank of Canada Act* is on the agenda of constitutional reform. We will be asked to consider whether the Bank's mandate should be changed, and whether the provinces — or a separate Quebec, if it comes to that — should have a greater role in its management. Given the international consensus I have just referred to, I do not think there is a great deal of room for regionalism in this area! In today's sadder-but-wiser international environment, conditions would need to be provocative indeed before a well-managed central bank deliberately set out to create monetary conditions supportive of inflation. Of course, a central bank has to deal with the unforeseeable. Shocks either on the demand or the supply side do require the exercise of discretion over a considerable range — for instance, in determining the length of time over which price stability, once disturbed, should be restored.

Central banking is simple in principle but exceedingly difficult in execution, and the costs of maintaining credible money can be embarrassingly high. If there is something to debate on this score, it should rather be whether Canada, including Quebec, should enter into a monetary union with the United States. There is certainly a case to be made that Canadians would experience equal or greater benefits, and lower costs, from simply adopting the U.S. dollar as their own. But the credibility of the Canadian dollar has by now largely been bought and paid for. For example, real interest rates on Canadian dollar securities do not seem to contain an excessive allowance for exchange risk. Given the respect in which the Bank of Canada is held and the promptness with which it has defended its monetary integrity when challenged, lenders appear to assign low prices to the risks associated with holding the Canadian dollar, and therefore the cost to Canadians of keeping the whole thing going seems likely to remain acceptably low. I am not as pessimistic about the prospects for U.S. inflation under the Fed as are Laidler and Robson. Like them, however, I do think Canada will do even better than the United States in getting inflation down over the next few years, so that, all in all, I think we would be better off to stay with the Canadian dollar at this time.

There can be only one monetary policy for Canada, and there really is only one condition it must meet for effectiveness: to concentrate on achieving and then maintaining, in the medium term, a trend of low or zero inflation. This means — and politicians and citizens need to understand this clearly — that *fiscal policy, whether at the federal or provincial level, bears no responsibility for managing the level of demand in the economy.* Indeed, if fiscal measures have the effect of strengthening or weakening demand inappropriately, then the central bank should be expected to take offsetting action through the financial and currency markets. Freed from responsibility for short-term demand management, federal and provincial fiscal policies can and should be directed fully toward achieving the efficiency and equity goals of the governments of the day. It is in this realm, not at the Bank of Canada, that greater coordination between provincial and federal policies would provide benefits. But since provincial and federal governments are often of different political stripes, the best we can hope for is that they will undertake their fiscal policies in full recognition of each other's (and the central bank's) likely reactions. Voters probably do understand quite well that to have two or three levels of government is to trade some rationality away in return for a good helping of creativity.

It appears that financial markets currently assign practically no likelihood to Quebec's separation. But if, by mischance, Quebec and ROC bargain so poorly with each other that separation does begin to appear likely, financial markets will quickly begin to assign non-trivial prices to the risks of economic loss to all parties. There are many aspects to this, but one is particularly important. Debts would become more costly to service, starting with the federal public debt and extending to everyone else's. Once Canada must rely on a foreign country, Quebec, to service a large part of its public debt, the risks that *all* debtholders run become more serious than they are today and will be priced accordingly. The inevitable difficulties in negotiating the allocation of the debt would make things even worse.

Since, for this and other reasons, reaching a divorce settlement would be very costly both to Quebec and to ROC, the governor of the central bank of the two countries — assuming that a monetary union had quickly been agreed to, and despite the qualms of Laidler and Robson, I *do* assume that — would find himself in an extraordinarily difficult situation. Flight by holders from Canadian and Quebec securities, anticipating greater risk of debt default, weaker economic health and higher taxes in both jurisdictions, and a greater risk of devaluation in the light of all of these, would put considerable downward pressure on the Canadian dollar, forcing the Bank of Canada to raise short-term interest rates, possibly sharply, in its defense.

Although other central banks would come to the Bank's aid in preventing disorderly exchange-market conditions, the fact that almost half of the federal debt is in the form of treasury bills or Canada Savings Bonds, and thus redeemable by the holder on short notice, would make a difficult situation into an agonizing one. Canada's large balance-of-payments deficit makes it even worse, because it puts foreign investors in the driver's seat — Canadians, including Quebecers, would have no option in the short run but to offer rates of return high enough not only to keep foreign lenders fully invested in their existing holdings of Canadian-dollar-denominated paper but to attract new money as well, on the order of $15 billion a year or more. As a result of having to deal quickly and decisively with these financial-market pressures, the level of short-term interest rates could well go high enough to impose a recession on Quebec and ROC, which would be especially vicious in interest-sensitive sectors.

These considerations obviously put tremendous pressure on the negotiators to renew federalism, and to do it quickly. Successful renewal, which would give the federal government a new lease on life, might permit the Bank of Canada to avoid taking the step of devaluation, and the crisis would pass. Alternatively, supposing negotiations were to end in separation, both Quebec and ROC might find that their joint currency had been devalued in the meantime and would probably want to start off their new lives by confirming that — in recognition of being mutually worse off. But there would be a great temptation for both new governments to collude in an over-devaluation, hoping to achieve a sharp drop in short-term interest rates by persuading lenders that the next exchange-rate move would be in the upward direction. With this risk in mind, until it became clear what trade arrangements and treaties the new countries could make with each other and with the United States, domestic and foreign savers would remain wary of the risks inherent in securities issued by the residents of what had once been Canada. Both new governments would be weaker credits, with reduced resources to draw upon but greater need to tax — a poisonous combination. The private sector in both areas, facing higher tax burdens and with weaker resources to meet them, would find that lenders would impose even greater increases in their borrowing costs.

In this unhappy setting, a strong central bank — that is, one which could effectively resist the political pressures to overdevalue — would prove to be an invaluable asset to both elements of the monetary union. If the central bank could persuade investors that securities denominated in Canadian dollars would retain most of their purchasing power in foreign-currency terms, it would contribute greatly to keeping the real cost of borrowing down on both sides of the Ottawa River. This does not mean only that the central bank would have to defend the currency aggressively against speculative attacks, but that it would have to continue to follow inflation-minimizing monetary policies.

A Note on the Desirability of a Separate Quebec Currency

William M. Scarth

Introduction

The purpose of this note is to offer comments on "Two Nations, One Money?" by David Laidler and William Robson. In this very clear essay, they argue that it is in the interest of both a sovereign Quebec (SQ) and "the Rest of Canada" (ROC) to preserve the existing monetary union, even if Quebec separates. While I agree with their basic conclusion, I have some concerns with a few specifics within their analysis. I will identify these points of debate as I review the issues below.

The note is organized as follows. In the next section, I summarize the six criteria by which Laidler and Robson judge the various possible monetary arrangements. Then, in the third section, I review how they score the two polar-case alternatives for SQ and ROC with respect to these criteria. The two basic alternatives are to maintain the existing currency union (with SQ using the ROC currency) or to create a separate SQ currency with a floating exchange-rate relationship with the ROC currency and the other world currencies.

One of the particularly appealing features of the Laidler/Robson paper is that they subject the all-Canada choice — between maintaining the separate Canadian dollar with a flexible exchange rate and simply using the U.S. dollar as Canada's currency — to the same scrutiny as the choice for SQ/ROC currency arrangements. After all, if one is to argue for a separate Canadian currency, and not for a separate SQ currency — and this is the joint recommendation of Laidler and Robson — one must be sure that one's reasoning is internally consistent. Thus, in the third section, I also summarize the arguments of Laidler and Robson regarding a separate Canadian dollar.

Concluding remarks are offered in the final section.

In a brief Appendix to this note, I explain an alternative and, I believe, more straightforward method for calculating seigniorage. Laidler and Robson highlight this issue, and provide considerable detail for their calculations. It turns out that seigniorage cannot be the central issue on which the basic policy choice depends. After all, when one is discussing such a fundamental change as the breakup of a country, it seems proper to question economists' traditional focus on marginal analysis. Nevertheless, it is useful to check by standard methods whether or not the seigniorage issue is dominated by other considerations.

Criteria for Judging Monetary Arrangements

Laidler and Robson rely on six criteria for judging alternative monetary arrangements:

(1) *An independent inflation policy,* which requires the ability to control the rate of issue of the nation's currency, and which is only possible if a nation has its own currency. This criterion favors an independent currency *if* it is reasonable to assume that the smaller country's own central bank would be able to impose a more controlled rate of money issue than would the central bank of the country whose currency the smaller country could use instead. Thus, for Canada, the key question is: Can the Bank of Canada fight inflation more diligently than the U.S. Federal Reserve? For SQ, the question is: Could its new central bank fight inflation more effectively than the Bank of Canada?

(2) *The ability to adjust in a less costly manner to permanent, real economic disturbances.* Such disturbances — a loss in the level of a country's competitiveness, for example — must result in excess unemployment for as long as it takes for the country's wage and price levels

to adjust downward by the required amount. Given downward rigidity in nominal contract structures, this process can be quite painful. *If* the level of the country's prices — measured from foreigners' point of view — can be lowered through a depreciation of its currency *without* that depreciation causing a significant increase in wages, then a flexible exchange rate can involve smaller transitional unemployment costs. This built-in stabilizer is not available with a fixed exchange rate — which is necessarily involved if another country's currency is used.

(3) *An increased ability to ensure financial liquidity.* Separate monetary institutions are needed if a country wants to be able to set up its own deposit-insurance schemes and lender-of-last-resort facilities.

(4) *The prevention of a loss of "seigniorage" revenue to the rest of the world.* Seigniorage refers to the fact that the institution issuing the monetary base which supports the country's payments system receives two forms of transfer payment. First, as new currency is issued in a growing economy, the issuing institution gets real goods and services in exchange for the newly issued — and essentially costless-to-produce — paper. Second, to the extent that the real purchasing power of the currency is shrinking at a rate equal to the amount of ongoing inflation, holders of the currency "receive" a negative yield on their asset equal to the rate of inflation. The issuer of the asset is the receiver of this yield. Clearly, if these transfers go to the central bank of another country — which must occur if that other country's currency is used — the seigniorage is lost. Domestic residents keep the seigniorage only if the money they use is the currency that their own central bank issues.

(5) *Lower transactions costs for international trade.* A country with its own currency and flexible exchange rates always faces an exchange-rate risk in unhedged foreign-exchange transactions. The country can avoid these transactions costs with the fixed exchange rate that is involved if it uses another country's currency.

(6) *A lower level for real interest rates.* Exchange-rate risk can also force a country's interest rates to be higher than (otherwise) comparable world rates. The possibility that its currency might depreciate forces some "risk premium" to be involved in the small country's yields. This risk premium can be avoided within a currency union.

Criteria (2), (3), and (4) represent arguments in favor of an independent currency with a flexible exchange rate. Criteria (5) and (6) lead to support for joining a currency union. The first — concerning inflation policy — can go either way, depending on how credible it is to assume that the small country's government and central bank can commit to the discipline required to maintain low inflation.

Clearly, then, one can defend a summary view only after securing some estimates of the magnitudes involved for each issue. In the next section, I review the empirical judgments that Laidler and Robson provide.

Which Criteria Are Most Important?

Laidler and Robson are uncertain about the importance of criterion (3). They argue that Canada needs to be free to intervene and to provide liquidity to the financial system in times of crisis. They further argue that, without expectations effects becoming destabilizing, SQ could get along with ROC's central bank performing a similar task for them. They admit that this institutional arrangement would require that the regulatory setup within SQ and ROC be coordinated. Also, since they acknowledge that Quebec and the federal government have already taken rather different approaches to the regulation of the financial sector, they are aware that this one part of their analysis is *not* a call for maintaining the status quo for financial institutions, and that there could be problems in this area if separation is not amicable.

The point about destabilizing expectations refers to the possibility that participants in financial markets could "force" SQ to create its own currency. For this to happen, all it takes is a widespread belief that some "other" market participants will reason in the following manner: Investors in SQ must attach some probability to a separate currency's coming into existence in the future, and to its being significantly devalued in its early days. To avoid this potential capital loss, investors would pull funds out of SQ, which would result in a recession there. To counter this financial crisis, SQ would have to create its own currency and then devalue it — and perhaps also impose wage and price controls — so that investors' initial fears would be realized. The more investors act on these fears, the more they force the very outcome that is the object of concern. But while Laidler and Robson acknowledge this vicious circle, they focus primarily on assessing which monetary arrangements are *desirable*, not which ones may *actually* emerge.

Laidler and Robson conclude that criteria (4), (5), and (6) are relatively unimportant. They estimate that the annual seigniorage costs for Canada of joining the U.S. currency union and for SQ of using the ROC dollar to be about one-quarter of 1 percent of (either Canada's or SQ's) GDP. While I question (in the Appendix) how Laidler and Robson estimate these costs, I do not argue with the bottom line that the amounts involved are small.[1]

If Canada were to join the U.S. currency union, the cost savings on international transactions are estimated to be between 0.17 and 0.40 of 1 percent of GDP. Laidler and Robson report a slightly wider band for the estimated transactions cost savings for SQ using the ROC dollar. These figures are fairly small and in any event they tend to cancel out the seigniorage gains of having an independent currency. Laidler and Robson argue that researchers have been unable to find a significant interest-rate risk premium that arises solely as a result of a country's small size.

By the process of elimination, then, the core of the preference by Laidler and Robson *for* a currency union between ROC and SQ and *against* one between Canada and the United States is based on

---

1 This conclusion is also supported by R.F. Lucas and B. Reid, "The Choice of Efficient Monetary Arrangements in the Post Meech Lake Era," University of Saskatchewan Working Paper 91-1 (Saskatoon, 1991).

criteria (1) and (2). Essentially, they argue that one can credibly predict a tough anti-inflation stand for the Bank of Canada, but not for either the U.S. Federal Reserve or the central bank of SQ. They also argue that a multi-industry economy such as Canada's satisfies the necessary conditions for the exchange rate to act as a built-in stabilizer better than does an economy that relies more heavily on just a few industries (as would SQ's).

Inflation

There are two parts to Laidler's and Robson's views on inflation; the first justifies their rejection of a separate SQ currency, while the second justifies their rejection of Canada's joining the U.S. currency area.

The first point is that, by their very nature, neither a *new* SQ currency nor a new SQ central bank would have a track record of credibility. As discussed above, participants in financial markets would operate on the presumption that the currency might be depreciated in the future — perhaps following a period of money-financed government spending in SQ. In an attempt to eliminate these expectations and to create an anticipation of eventual appreciation instead, the SQ central bank would be tempted to keep the SQ currency undervalued for a significant time. But this policy of pegging the exchange rate destroys the advantages of a flexible rate, and the resulting balance-of-payments deficit that would be forced on the ROC would cause recession there. This represents an important implementation problem for the separate SQ currency option.

Laidler's and Robson's second point on inflation is that the Bank of Canada can be expected to have more credibility than the U.S. Federal Reserve in the future, since the U.S. financial system is currently very shaky and since there is such a strong temptation for the United States to inflate away its large external debt that is denominated in U.S. dollars. While Laidler and Robson admit that Canada has had a higher inflation rate than the United States through most of the postwar period, they nevertheless argue that the two countries' relative inflation performance may be reversed during the coming decade. My own guess is that the Canadian authorities may be satisfied when Canada's inflation rate is no greater than that of the United States. It must be remembered that the Canadian government debt level represents a large problem, and that there is ongoing pressure to monetize whatever portion of the current deficit that does not lead to "too much" inflation.

More generally, I would argue that all remarks about the credibility of future monetary policy in SQ, ROC, and the United States should be viewed as speculative, since no one can be sure how fiscal policy in SQ or ROC might be different after a fundamental political change. Even alternative monetary policies can induce rather different degrees of fiscal discipline. Given the explosive nature of the Canadian government's debt-service obligations, more research is needed on how to control inflation *without* having this problem emerge.

Incidently, Laidler and Robson make a rather selective reference to the large benefits of fighting inflation — presumably to stress how the monetary arrangement that delivers the lower inflation rate should be viewed as having a big advantage over other institutional arrangements. To be complete however, if they wish to point out *permanent* favorable effects of lower inflation on productivity, they should also point out the *permanent* effects of reducing inflation on unemployment, for which there is just as much evidence.[2] I am not arguing that low inflation is not worth pursuing; I am simply noting that the net benefits of totally eliminating inflation are much smaller than bringing inflation down to a low level,[3] and that if the United States can maintain a low and stable rate of inflation, then joining the U.S. currency union can be defended. In short, I find the arguments by Laidler and Robson against a separate SQ currency quite convinc-

---

2 See P. Fortin, "The Phillips Curve, Macroeconomic Policy, and the Welfare of Canadians," *Canadian Journal of Economics* 24 (1991).

3 See W.M. Scarth, "Fighting Inflation: Are the Costs of Getting to Zero Too High?" in Robert C. York, ed., *Taking Aim: The Debate on Zero Inflation*, Policy Study 10 (Toronto: C.D. Howe Institute, 1990), pp. 81–103.

ing, while I find their case for a separate Canadian currency less compelling. Nevertheless, I favor a separate Canadian currency for a different reason. I think that a flexible form of monetarism — such as a policy of nominal income targeting, not strict money growth targeting — is required if one is to control *both* inflation *and* the fiscal debt dynamics,[4] and that such a monetary policy requires a floating exchange rate.

Unemployment

As to keeping short-run changes in employment to a minimum following real economic disturbances, there are several reasons why a floating exchange rate does not provide as much insulation for a small, open economy — such as Canada's — as Robert Mundell predicted in his 1963 analysis:[5]

- First, supply-side effects of exchange-rate changes are important — for example, with wage rates tied to the cost of living, a domestic currency depreciation has a direct stagflationary effect.
- Second, there is the phenomenon known as the "Dutch disease", whereby an economy with two distinct sectors can be forced to undergo significant resource reallocations as a result of an exchange-rate change. For example, a rise in primary goods prices can lead to a large appreciation in the domestic currency of a resource-rich country, with the result that a painful profit squeeze is imposed on its manufacturing sector.
- Third, exchange-rate "overshooting" occurs when other macroeconomic variables move sluggishly, forcing the exchange rate to move more in the short run than it will have to in the longer run, following various disturbances.

---

4 See W.M. Scarth, "Alternative Monetary Rules, Fiscal Discipline, and Macroeconomic Stability" (McMaster University, Hamilton, Ont., 1991, Mimeographed).

5 R.A. Mundell, "Capital Mobility and Stabilization Policy under Fixed and Flexible Exchange Rates," *Canadian Journal of Economics and Political Science* 29 (1963).

- Fourth, there is the optimal-currency-area consideration: the argument in favor of a flexible exchange rate applies best when the country corresponds to an economic region — high factor mobility within its borders and low factor mobility across its borders. Economists do not know how fundamental political change may affect factor-mobility patterns.

Of these four reasons why a flexible exchange rate can fail to provide a significant degree of built-in stability, Laidler and Robson focus only on the first. They argue that the direct supply-side effect of the exchange rate should be much more pronounced in a small economy in which it is more obvious to wage earners how important the exchange rate is for the cost of living.

As part of their argument in this regard, Laidler and Robson present a scatter diagram that illustrates the relationship between the size of an economy and the variability of its real exchange rate. But this analysis involves just manufactured goods prices (not resource prices) and it abstracts from external events that affect the exchange rate through the capital account. The first of these limitations may have been important for the United Kingdom during the periods following dramatic oil price changes, while the second may be significant for interpreting recent U.S. and Japanese interaction. If these three countries were removed from the scatter diagram, the relationship illustrated there would be much less clear cut. To avoid these concerns, I prefer to acknowledge the relevance of the other three arguments given above, which lead to the view that a flexible exchange rate may not act as an important built-in stabilizer. The net result of doing this strengthens the case against a separate SQ currency, while weakening the case in favor of a separate Canadian currency.

A final point regarding built-in stability is worth making: Canada's exchange-rate regime fundamentally influences the effects of provincial stabilization policy.[6]

---

6 This issue is pursued in W.M. Scarth, "Coordination Issues with Provincial Stabilization Policy," in a forthcoming volume on fiscal policy in The Canada Round series.

Conclusion

Laidler and Robson argue that the status quo for Canadian monetary arrangements should be preserved, even if Quebec separates. Their essay is clearly written, and they defend their conclusions cogently. I support their rejection both of a separate SQ currency and of Canada's joining the U.S. currency union. My preference for a separate Canadian dollar and a floating exchange rate is somewhat weaker than theirs, and it is based (to some extent) on different arguments. But these remarks concern the details of the analysis; the disagreements that I have are at the margin.

Appendix

An Alternative Method for Calculating Seigniorage

In this appendix, I explain an alternative method for calculating seigniorage. For a small country with a separate currency, a flexible exchange rate, and no taxation of foreigners, the full-equilibrium version of the government's financing constraint can be written as:

$$g + [r(1 - t) - p - n]b = t + m(p + n),$$

where b is the ratio of government bonds to real GDP, g is the ratio of real government spending on goods and services to real GDP, m is the ratio of the real monetary base to real GDP, n is the percentage growth rate of real GDP, p is the domestic inflation rate, r is the domestic nominal rate of interest, and t is the proportional tax rate on factor earnings and bond interest income.[*]

The uses of government funds are direct expenditures on goods and interest payments on the debt, and the sources of government funds are direct taxes and the implicit tax levied on the holders of domestic money. There are two components to the latter: the negative yield earned on pre-existing money holdings, equal in absolute value to pm, and the amount of real goods and services commanded by the new issue of money, which is required to keep the money-GDP ratio constant as the economy grows, equal to nm. The sum of these two component levies is the seigniorage revenue accruing to the domestic government, since the $m(p + n)$ term simply does not appear when the government does not have currency issue as a financing option — as is the case when the small open economy is part of a wider currency union.

---

[*] For a full explanation and derivation of this government budget constraint, see W.M. Scarth, "Debt and Deficits in an Open Economy," *Journal of International Money and Finance* 7 (1988).

To be complete, one should evaluate the material welfare of the small country's citizens by looking through the "veil" of government, and calculating the effect on the citizens' full-equilibrium consumption possibilities — denoted by c — that occurs as a result of joining a currency union. In an earlier paper,* I derive an expression for c, and by following the argument presented there, the reader can verify that

$$a - b = m(p + n),$$

where a is the value of c that obtains when the small country has its own currency and a flexible exchange rate, while b is the value of c that obtains when the small country joins the currency union. Hence, one can be confident that $m(p + n)$ is an appropriate measure of seigniorage. (There is an additional one-time loss in entering a currency union — that of acquiring the initial stock of "foreign" currency to replace the previous domestic monetary base; I am not considering this issue here.)

This seigniorage measure can be calculated without needing information on such things as the money-demand elasticities on which Laidler and Robson rely. In 1990, the Canadian monetary base (measured as a proportion of GDP) was 0.034 . Thus, with $m = 0.034$, $p = 0.06$, and $n = 0.03$, seigniorage is approximately 0.31 percent of GDP — an estimate that is slightly bigger than that of Laidler and Robson.

---

* Ibid.

A Comment

Bernard Fortin

In their clear and comprehensive paper, David Laidler and William Robson have provided both a normative and a positive analysis of issues regarding monetary arrangements between a sovereign Quebec (SQ) and "the Rest of Canada" (ROC). In their normative analysis, which constitutes the most important part of the paper (sections 2 and 3), they evaluate the costs and benefits of four monetary options from the point of view of each region. These options are:

(1) an SQ currency with a floating exchange rate;
(2) an SQ currency pegged to the ROC or the U.S. dollar;
(3) unilateral use of the ROC dollar by SQ; and
(4) use of the ROC dollar by SQ, with SQ's participation in a common monetary policy.

The authors' main message is that a monetary union between SQ and ROC with a joint central bank (option 4) is the welfare-maximizing option from the standpoint of both SQ and ROC. Moreover, option 3 is the second-best arrangement, while a separate SQ currency with a flexible exchange rate (option 1) is the least desirable option. From their positive analysis of the political dynamics of the breakup of the Canadian federation (section 4), however, Laidler and Robson argue that it is a real possibility that SQ may choose to adopt the most unpleasant option.

Normative Analysis

I fundamentally agree with the general conclusions of the normative analysis that Laidler and Robson present in the paper, which, by and large, confirm those advanced in most research studies written on the subject. Interestingly, their conclusions are also in basic agreement with recent official documents published in Quebec — such as the Bélanger-Campeau Commission Report — that discuss the best monetary arrangements between SQ and ROC. Two points, however, deserve particular attention.

First, in their analysis of option 2, Laidler and Robson argue that initially pegging a newly created SQ currency at an artificially low level in terms of the ROC dollar would inflict short-run economic damage on ROC and would create domestic inflation in SQ in the long run. This argument seems to miss the basic point that the introduction of a new currency combined with a firm commitment by the central bank to peg its exchange rate at a given value is analogous to implementing a monetary reform — such as the replacement of old francs with new francs in France in 1960. In other words, it is equivalent to a change in the unit of account used in the country. Thus, in principle, the exchange rate of an SQ currency could be fixed initially at any value in terms of the ROC dollar without influencing the real value of contracts made in SQ or in ROC. For instance, the SQ central bank could choose to fix the exchange rate of an SQ currency at ROC$10. In that case, the value of all contracts denominated in ROC dollars would simply have to be divided by ten to be expressed in terms of the new SQ currency. Of course, this reasoning is valid only as long as the commitment of the SQ central bank to peg the SQ exchange rate is fully credible in the markets. In this sense, I agree with Laidler and Robson that credibility is one of the most important concerns that would arise in the event of the introduction of an SQ currency.

Related to this point is the authors' analysis of the impact of the creation of an SQ currency on the level of seigniorage held by the ROC monetary authorities. They argue that ROC would then have to cancel about one-quarter of outstanding Canadian dollar banknotes and coins. This would deprive the ROC monetary authorities of seigniorage — that is, the profits of the central bank — amounting to some $360 million annually over the next decade. This analysis, however, does not take into account the fact that, in the short run, the SQ central bank would probably have to hold a large part of its foreign reserves in Canadian dollars in order to be able to react against eventual speculative movements against the SQ currency coming from ROC. These reserves would also help to solve problems of credibility that the SQ monetary authorities likely would face. In this event, it is clear that the loss of SQ seigniorage would be much less important than Laidler and Robson predict. Thus, if the SQ monetary authorities decided to adopt a 100 percent reserve coefficient in Canadian dollars, the creation of the SQ currency would not as such involve any reduction in ROC seigniorage.

Positive Analysis

While the authors' cost-benefit analysis of the monetary options of SQ and ROC is generally thoughtful and persuasive, I found their positive analysis of the likely monetary arrangements in the event of Quebec separation much less convincing. In a sense, this is not surprising, since there are very few historical examples of highly integrated democracies breaking up that one might use to make predictions. Therefore, venturing to predict the monetary consequences of an SQ is a highly risky activity.

Laidler and Robson argue that negotiations between SQ and ROC over the maintenance of an economic union as well as the division of federal net assets are likely to be acrimonious. Therefore, nationalist special-interest groups in both SQ and ROC would see their influence increase sharply. This, they argue, would induce the governments of SQ and ROC to be uncooperative about their future economic and monetary arrangements. One likely outcome of such a political process could be the introduction of an SQ currency. Moreover, given investors' lack of confidence about the stability of this currency, the SQ central bank could have an incentive to devaluate and to introduce capital controls in order to stimulate the SQ economy artificially and to prevent an outflow of capital from SQ.

In my view, there are many reasons why this unpleasant scenario is unlikely to occur.[1] First, even if an acrimonious breakup increases the influence of some nationalist interest groups in both SQ and ROC, such groups are unlikely to dominate the strength of financial and commercial groups that have a strong interest in maintaining an economic and monetary union between SQ and ROC. In fact, since both SQ and ROC would share the risks and transactions costs associated with the introduction of an SQ currency, while its benefits are mostly concentrated in SQ, this might give SQ potentially important bargaining strength in negotiating a monetary union with ROC.

A related point concerns the crucial importance of the dynamic process of creating confidence in a new currency. Lessons from history[2] show that the credibility of a new currency is fragile and that it may take a long time to become established in the markets. In order to minimize the duration of this period, the central bank has, in the short run, every incentive to stabilize its exchange rate. This implies, however, that, during this period, the need to peg the exchange rate would severely limit the bank's ability to use monetary policy to reach domestic objectives. Stated differently, the domestic benefits of introducing a new currency will appear only in the long run. This analysis has two implications. First, an SQ government elected with a short-run mandate would have few incentives to create a SQ currency, even in the event of an acrimonious breakup, since its benefits would appear only in the long run — say, after five to ten years. Second, were an SQ government nevertheless to introduce a new currency, it would not find it desirable to devaluate the currency's external value in the short run in order to establish its credibility

---

1 The description of such a pessimistic scenario is not new; Richard Lipsey discussed a quite similar one as early as 1977. See Richard G. Lipsey, "The Relation between Political and Economic Separation: A Pessimistic View" (Paper presented at the Conference on the Future of the Canadian Federation, University of Toronto, October 1977).

2 See, for example, Henri-Paul Rousseau, "L'intégration politique: est-elle nécessaire à l'intégration monétaire?" in Claude Montmarquette et al., *Économie du Québec et choix politiques* (Montréal: Les Presses de l'Université du Québec, 1979).

in the markets. These arguments may explain why Ireland, for example, waited more than seven years after its independence from the United Kingdom before creating its own currency, and more than 50 years before unpegging its value from the pound sterling.

The preceding analysis suggests that, in the long run, SQ nevertheless might find it desirable to create its own currency and to use it for domestic purposes. However, the increasing globalization of markets and the international pressure for free trade and less regulation represent forces that could counteract this eventuality. These forces partly explain why countries such as those of the European Community are contemplating the possibility of forming a monetary union by the end of the century (the Delors Plan). In this respect, it is also clear that the political viability of this union will require the existence of a supranational central bank with representatives of participant countries in order to induce each of them to accept the common monetary policy. One wonders whether this type of institution would be politically conceivable in the case of SQ and ROC. One way to make such an arrangement more acceptable would be to regionalize the common central bank, along the lines of a proposal put forward recently by Peter Howitt.[3] In fact, Howitt makes a convincing case for such a reform, whether or not Quebec secedes from Canada.

---

3 See Peter Howitt, "Constitutional Reform and the Bank of Canada" (Paper presented to the conference, "Economic Dimensions of Constitutional Change," sponsored by the John Deutsch Institute for the Study of Economic Policy, Kingston, Ont., June 4–6, 1991, Mimeographed).

The Contributors

Lloyd C. Atkinson is Executive Vice-President and Chief Economist, Bank of Montreal.

Bernard Fortin is Professor of Economics, Université Laval.

John Grant is Chief Economist, Wood Gundy Inc.

David E.W. Laidler is an Adjunct Scholar at the C.D. Howe Institute and Professor of Economics, University of Western Ontario.

William B.P. Robson is a Senior Policy Analyst at the C.D. Howe Institute and Canadian Director of Research for the Canadian-American Committee.

William M. Scarth is Professor of Economics, McMaster University.

Members of the
C.D. Howe Institute[*]

[*] The views expressed in this publication are those of the authors, and do not necessarily reflect the opinions of the Institute's members.

ScotiaMcLeod Inc.
Sears Canada Inc.
Hugh D. Segal
Anthony A. Shardt
Sharwood and Company
Shell Canada Limited
Sherritt Gordon Limited
Sidbec-Dosco Inc.
Smith, Lyons, Torrance, Stevenson &
    Mayer
Le Soleil
Southam Inc.
Derek J. Speirs
Standard Life Assurance Company
Stikeman, Elliott, Advocates
Strategico Inc.
Sun Life Assurance Company of Canada
Suncor Inc.
Swiss Bank Corporation (Canada)
Teck Corporation
Laurent Thibault
Thomson Newspapers Limited

3M Canada Inc.
The Toronto Dominion Bank
Toronto Star Newspaper Limited
The Toronto Stock Exchange
TransAlta Utilities Corporation
TransCanada PipeLines Limited
Trimac
Trizec Corporation Ltd.
Robert J. Turner
Unilever Canada Inc.
Urgel Bourgie Limitée
Manon Vennat
VIA Rail Canada Inc.
J.H. Warren
Tom M. Waterland
West Fraser Timber Co. Ltd.
Westcoast Energy Inc.
George Weston Limited
M.K. Wong & Associates Ltd.
Wood Gundy Limited
Xerox Canada Inc.
Zurich Life Insurance of Canada

Honorary Members

G. Arnold Hart
David Kirk
Paul H. Leman

A.M. Runciman
J. Ross Tolmie, Q.C.

Publications in
"The Canada Round"

The Economics of Constitutional Renewal

How Shall We Govern the Governor? A Critique of the Governance of the Bank of Canada, The Canada Round 1, by David E.W. Laidler (38 pp.; May 1991).

In Praise of Renewed Federalism, The Canada Round 2, by Thomas J. Courchene (102 pp.; July 1991). This publication is also available in French.

(Forthcoming)

The Division of Spending and Taxing Powers, by Irene Ip and Jack Mintz, with John Richards, Jean-Michel Cousineau, Robin Boadway, André Raynauld, and Claude Forget.

The Social Charter, by Lars Osberg and Shelly Phipps, with John Myles, John Richards, and François Vaillancourt.

Fiscal Policy: Deficits and Regional Coordination, by Herbert Grubel, with William Scarth, Douglas Purvis, and Jan Winter.

Eastern and Western Perspectives, by Douglas May and Dane Rowlands, with Edward Chambers, Michael Percy, Norman Cameron, Derek Hum, and Wayne Simpson.

Resource Mobility and the Economic Union, by Fred Lazar, with David Brown and Daniel Schwanen.

Summary and Synthesis, by Richard Lipsey and John McCallum